Diving Blind into Danger

By Owen Boyle

I hope you enjoy my book. I sure enjoyed writing it.

Owen Boyle

Copyright © 2016 Owen Boyle
All rights reserved.

Acknowledgements

This book has taken 5 years to complete and for all of those years, my family has been interested and supportive. As the book neared completion, we would gather for a family get-together and someone would read a chapter out loud. Their input has been invaluable. They let me know what they liked, what made their hearts pound and also, gave constructive criticism when they didn't understand some of the technical descriptions of the hazards involved in diving down through complicated structures in totally black water. Criticisms which I took to heart and hopefully, corrected.

My wife, Fleur, typed the entire manuscript, our daughter Linda Huhndorf, drew the picture for the chapter "Getting Sid Out" and the wonderful cover for my book. Our son Matt Boyle spent many hours preparing the manuscript for publication. Thanks also to Debbie Boyle who used her photographic skills enhancing the photos used in the book.

Thank you to my whole family for all your encouragement and help….. Thanks to Tom and Jenny Martin, Linda and Mike Huhndorf, Matt and Debbie Boyle, who put in their time listening and reacting, and David Boyle who, though in Texas, read the chapters and offered his valuable opinions as well. Your encouragement kept me writing.

My appreciation and high regard to Steve Abel and Kevin Hanley of Alaska Piledrivers and Divers Union Local 2520, who have provided training and safety leadership for divers and all union members over the years. They sent an excerpt from my book to the Northwest Carpenters & Divers local union which was published in the Union newsletter ...Thank you. It was great seeing a chapter of mine in print.

Thanks to my friend, Tom Ulrich, who encouraged me to keep plugging away at writing my book. I was always very proud to work for American Marine established by Scott Vuillemot, owner and president of American Marine and Tom Ulrich, Vice President. They have a deserved reputation for outstanding safety practices in this dangerous business. I always knew their support was behind the men working for them. Any time an urgent need arose on the job, I would call Tom and he'd get it for me. They have been the best to work for.

Finally, I want to pay tribute to Gene Cleary, one of the best diving partners and friends I've ever had and I miss him.

Table of Contents

Chapter 1   The Adventurous Baker Platform---7

Chapter 2   The Grayling---------------------------21

Chapter 3   Cutting Off Baker's Pontoons------32

Chapter 4   Getting Sid Out-----------------------40

Chapter 5   Hazardous Adventures--------------51

Chapter 6   Ice---62

Chapter 7   Wodeco II----------------------------79

Chapter 8   Steelhead-----------------------------89

DIVING BLIND INTO DANGER

Even as a boy, I always had a powerful admiration for Deep Sea Divers. The picture of that manly fellow in that rugged looking gear, calmly watching the tender starting to lower the helmet over his head inspired me. The helmet cranks down over the breast plate, and is twisted into the locked position. The diver walks over to the edge of the derrick barge. He grasps the descending line in his right hand and holds his diving hose in his left. "Are we ready?" he will ask over the dive radio. "Ready," the tender will reply. The diver will leap off the barge feet first into the water and descend out of sight.

I was twenty nine when I finally became that diver.

CHAPTER 1---The Adventurous Baker Platform

September 13, 1965 I was in Anchorage, Alaska boarding a helicopter for a 50 mile trip down Cook Inlet. I was going to a diving barge anchored next to a brand new platform named Baker to begin my first diving job in the Cook Inlet.

The upper Inlet is roughly 15 to 20 miles wide and about 60 miles long. On the east side is a huge spruce and birch tree forest dotted with beautiful lakes of all sizes. The Chugach Mountains can be seen in the far distance. On the west side, running close and parallel to the Inlet is the Alaska Range....ruggedly steep and jagged. Some peaks are over 10,000 feet high. Nearby Mount Redoubt is a recently active volcano. There are numerous big swift rivers which come down out of the mountains into the upper Cook Inlet. These rivers carry tremendous quantities of silt into the Inlet waters and create a diver's work arena of absolutely zero visibility....top to bottom! I soon learned that even when a very experienced Inlet diver leaps off the side of the dive barge into that black water, he is startled and shocked by his sudden blindness.

I regretted that this wonderful sightseeing trip came to a close when a helicopter landed on the derrick barge anchored alongside platform Baker. I'd heard a lot about the Inlet from Gene Cleary who had been my diving partner in California. He had recently moved to Alaska and his stories about the work opportunities lured me to follow, but I wasn't prepared for what I saw when I got off the helicopter. Grey water rushing by the derrick barge sending all of the big anchor cables into fast and furious

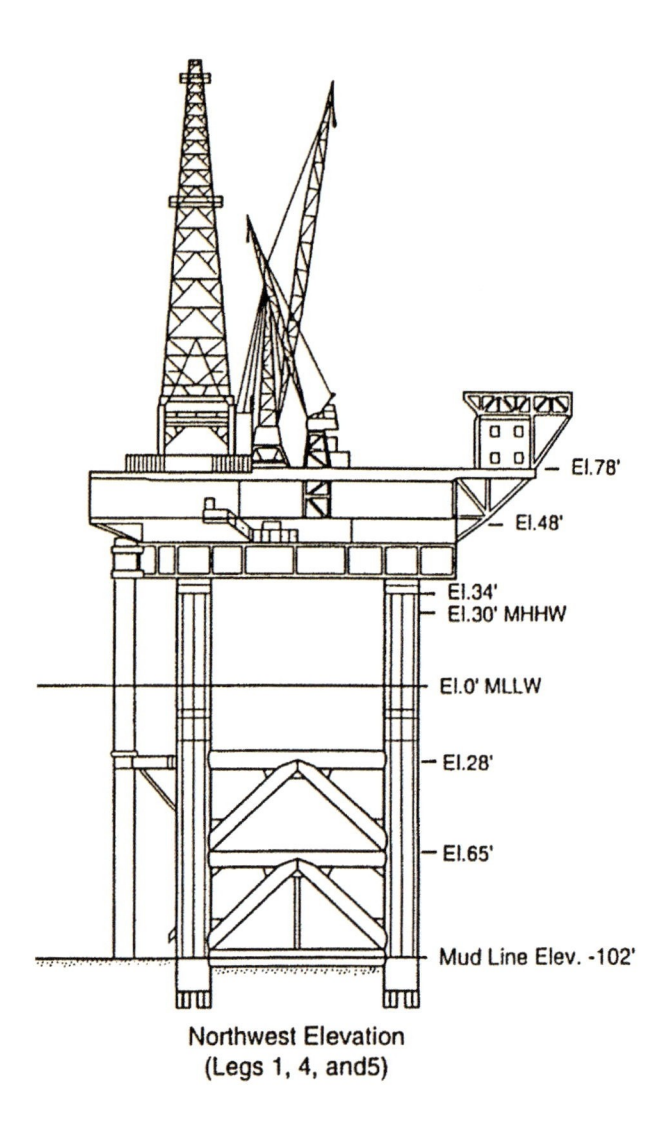

El.78'
El.48'
El.34'
El.30' MHHW
El.0' MLLW
El.28'
El.65'
Mud Line Elev. -102'

Northwest Elevation
(Legs 1, 4, and 5)

Compiled by Belmar Engineering, Redondo Beach, CA for
the Cook Inlet Regional Citizens Advisory Council

looking vibrations....a powerful, violent but minute shivering. This dramatic visual indicator of the tremendous tidal current power was ominous to see.

The divers take turns-alternately diving one tide and then standing by for the other diver on the next tide. In the 1960's we dove in the old fashion "deep sea gear," commonly known simply as "heavy gear." Commercial deep sea dive suits are called diving dresses hence the term "the diver is dressed in." Modern neoprene dive suits are also now made for "heavy gear" helmets.

That afternoon, the good old heavy gear was laid out on the deck of McDermott's derrick barge No. 7 and I began my 40 year career as an Inlet diver. Baker had only recently been positioned onto the sea floor when I joined Gene and the crew in September, 1965. The crew had just begun to realize what a diving adventure this platform was going to be. It was moderately deep, about 130 feet on a high tide and that usually meant decompression time for the diver. To avoid the "bends," decompression water stops are specified at various shallow depths. The length of time at a stop depends on the depth and the duration of the dive. But the Inlet's fast changing tidal currents usually preclude water stops. This means that the diver must take his "stops" in a recompression chamber on deck. From the moment the diver gets out of the water, he must get into the recompression chamber, and put under pressure within 5 minutes.

Gene took first dive of our shift. The mission was to inspect one of the four 3 inch diameter 200 foot long cables that had been used to pull and rotate the platform into the proper orientation before setting it onto the bottom. These cables had been shackled into big pad-eyes (metal plates with a hole) welded near the top of each leg and perpendicular to it. When the survey team was satisfied with the platform's location, the legs were purposely flooded in a way that caused the platform to reorient itself from a horizontal to a vertical posture in the water. The flooding then continued and the platform descended to the sea floor.

The tug boat crew tied a long divers' descending buoy line on each of the four cables before throwing the cables over the side. The oil company supervisor was concerned about the cables fouling later pipelines and anode sled cables. The divers were instructed to inspect the cables.

Gene checked the first one. He determined that it was clear of the platform but very close to it. Then he checked a couple of other things the engineers wanted to know about. I was completely "dressed-in," as the stand-by diver must be and stood right next to Jim Dominish, Gene's tender, while he listened to Gene on the dive radio. Jim checked everything constantly: the tide action, the diver's depth gauge, the anchor wire's vibrations, the down line…was it still vibrating? He scanned off to the sides of the boat, looking for signs of the tide changing…or a sudden maverick rip current.

Near dive's end, Jim gave Gene a hose check, pulling sharply on the diver's hose to make sure it was clear and told him he had about 5 minutes left and to head back to the cable. Gene quickly found the cable and began his ascent. By then the tide was definitely starting to turn. Jim then had to decide if Gene had time to take his specified 30 foot water stop before surfacing and going into the recompression chamber for his surface decompression to avoid the "bends".

No, the tide was picking up too fast. Gene would have to take his decompression stop in the boat's recompression chamber. Jim told Gene to come right to the surface, and then made a note in his dive log to increase chamber stop times to compensate for the omitted water stop. As soon as Gene surfaced, the hose tender pulled him over to the dive ladder.

There is an extremely important fact about surface decompression that dive crews have learned to deal with in order to prevent any possibility of the bends (decompression sickness). The time span from when the diver reaches the surface until he is back under pressure in the chamber must not exceed five minutes! This is accomplished by speedy team work.

When Gene stepped off the ladder onto the deck, he was simultaneously besieged by five men. Al Wickman, who became my tender, removed his helmet while two other men removed the weight belt. Meanwhile, two others were removing his ankle weights and galoshes. Gene and Jim rushed to the chamber and climbed quickly into the outer lock. The hatch was slammed shut and Jim opened the valve between the inner and outer locks of the chamber. The inner lock had been previously "blown down" to a water depth pressure at 60 feet so a very fast outer lock pressurization began immediately…in less than five minutes from surfacing. This is usual. Only rarely is the five minute rule violated. If it is, the diver must take a much longer Treatment Table decompression.

Jim removed Gene's breast plate and helped pull off his suit, while the outer lock was being pressurized. The two locks soon equalized at 30 feet. Gene entered the inner lock and slammed the hatch shut. Jim then opened the exhaust valve to depressurize the outer lock and take it to the surface. He then emerged from the chamber to run Gene's decompression. He added some time to the stops because of the omitted water decompression. Gene emerged from the chamber in about 90 minutes and said he was feeling fine.

Now we started setting up for my first dive in the Inlet. I had dived in black water and fast water before....but never simultaneously. The zero visibility diver quickly learns to pay attention to the heightened sensitivity of his other senses: touch and feel especially.

Gene gave me some last minute pointers. "We always start diving when the tide is still running. This gives you early current directions, either ebbing or flooding...but that doesn't last too long. If you're lucky the tide may go completely slack, but that doesn't happen too often. Sometimes it never stops. It will slow down a bit and start going sideways....at right angles to the usual current flow directions. And sometimes the tide will already have changed direction 180 degrees and started its new current direction buildup from the bottom."

These are all the things Gene and Jim explained to me yesterday, and I was really mulling them over today. High tides are about 130 feet deep at Baker. Lows are about 115 feet. Low tide dive times are of shorter duration than highs, and they turn faster. At this platform they often turn sideways, heading westerly for a while before they turn and start flooding.

I had examined a platform schematic and was impressed by the three levels of bracings between the legs. The cable I was to inspect was on the leg furthest away from the barge. A line from the surface to the work is always called the "down line." This line led down along the outside of the leg close to the barge, and then over to the far leg and the cable. It would be a "bit of a jaunt", but I was looking forward to it.

Time to go. Al put on my helmet and then got on the dive radio. "Looks good up here," he said. I saw that my hose tender had good slack in his hands. I held onto my air hose with my left hand about 5 feet back from the helmet, grasped the down line loosely in my right hand, and jumped off the barge feet first. I had jumped in a little early all right. The minute I entered the water the current tried to flag my legs out sideways. I quickly got one leg around the down line and started pulling myself down, hand over hand.

"Leaving surface," I announced to Al. He acknowledged and entered the time on his dive sheet. Down I went. The deeper I got the harder it was to pull myself down. The current pushing on the vertical hose exerted an upward pull vector, so I had to frequently request extra slack in my hose to get it bellying out behind to reduce the up-pull. I finally got to the bottom and grabbed the heavy cable the down line was tied to. I hung on the cable with both hands and told Al to tight-line my hose. They started pulling. It took a little time but they finally got my hose snugged up somewhat vertically. "Okay Al, I'm going out the cable, start slacking me." He agreed and I started off, laboriously. The tide was still running out and I had to buck into it. The backward tide pull on my hose slowed me down, too.

The cable finally started coming off the bottom and then my helmet banged into the leg. The Inlet diver usually travels crouching and leaning forward. Thank goodness for those tough old brass helmets…..dents and all. I felt around the leg a bit and then started climbing up the cable. I climbed further up this cable, which was coming alongside the leg now and I felt the lower four foot diameter horizontal brace going from this leg back to the leg near the barge. I felt the gusset on top of this brace and felt the 5 foot vertical diagonal joining the leg just above the horizontal (see schematic).

I knew the diameters from the schematic but those braces sure felt big down here in the fast black water. I kept climbing up the cable. It was now almost vertical and at a steady distance about a foot out from the leg. I told all this to Al. He had been watching the pneumofathometer and knew I was ascending. He told me he was worried about hose hang-ups, not only on this leg, but on the leg back by the barge. He told me not to go any higher. I really appreciated his watchful caution. Anyway, I felt sure the cable was probably leading right straight up the leg to the big pad-eye hole it was shackled into.

Just for the fun of it, I tried to man handle the cable. I braced myself against the leg and pushed with all my might. I might have moved it 3 or4 inches. It was not only heavy, but was also restrained by sea floor friction. My survey had shown that the cable was not fouled anywhere on the platform, so I thought I'd "look around a little," so to speak. I came back down the cable. When I got to the bottom I was a bit away from the leg and noticed the current had slowed, but had shifted 90 degrees. I didn't notice it up higher because the leg had provided a protective lee.

About then, Al told me the current had turned sideways and was now heading west away from the platform and would soon accelerate. That was good news for my hose, anyway. Al checked my hose. I could feel two strong pulls and it felt unencumbered. Al told me he wanted me to start working my way back. As I did so, the tenders constantly retrieved the slack in my hose and kept it comfortably snug. I got back to the down line and told Al I was ready to come up.

He checked my hose and told me I had a short 10 foot water stop and that no chamber time was required. "Up on the diver, "he said. "Let me know when you leave the bottom." My first Inlet dive went well. I was pleased and relieved to have that first one done. On tomorrow morning's high tide, Gene would check another cable.

Our next shift was on a pleasant Alaskan Indian Summer day. We worked setting up all the gear and then tight-lined the down line to the third cable. The down line led almost horizontally over to the inside of the leg nearest to the barge. It was either hung up somehow on the leg or it was going over the top horizontal brace to the inside of the platform. Gene jumped in. The current carried him over there quickly. Gene paused briefly. "It's going down inside the platform. Slack my hose," he said. The top horizontal was 7 feet in diameter and caused a lot of skin friction on the hose. As he descended, he said something about finding the cable near the leg and following it down. He was having trouble getting slack against all the friction from the three different horizontal braces and their vertical diagonals. He finally got to the bottom and said he was starting to trace out the cable but that it seemed fouled.

Jim told Gene we wanted to check his hose. Gene said OK. The hose tender pulled it tight. Jim asked, "Do you feel that?" Gene said, "No."

"We are going to pull harder. Are you ready?" Jim put two other men on the hose. All of them pulled as hard as they could. They could not get an inch of slack.

I watched those three strong men pulling as hard as they could on Gene's fouled air hose. That was a scary sight. Two guys helped me get my weight belt on. Al moved my dive radio right over next to Jim and Gene's radio. We decided that using two separate radios was the best way to go. Our tenders would relay information back and forth. There would be a time delay and it would be awkward, but it was simpler and less confusing than having both divers on one dive radio.

By this time my helmet was back on and I was ready to go. I jumped over the side with my right hand sliding down Gene's hose which became my down line. I followed it over the big 7 ft. diameter horizontal brace. The hose was real tight against it. I didn't want to put any more slack into his hose, so I finger gripped his hose tight while I got over the brace and down inside the platform. While I was heading down into that black, zero visibility water, I asked Al what was going on with Gene, is he OK? Al replied that Gene and Jim had been talking a lot but that he hadn't heard exactly what the problem was.

I kept on going down and ran into a vertical diagonal brace. It was another big seven footer and Gene's hose was running down alongside of it. I followed his hose down the brace and asked Al again about what was happening with Gene. Al said he still couldn't understand what the problem was. I couldn't imagine that they didn't have the problem defined by now and I was really getting worried. I got to thinking that perhaps some of the cable he was following had lodged precariously on a lower brace and had fallen down on him or his hose.

Then I came to the place where the vertical diagonal joined the leg. The top of the middle 5 ft. diameter horizontal also joined the leg at the bottom of the vertical diagonal. A big gusset plate at this large vertex area made a good hand hold. At this spot I was about 40 feet directly above Gene.

I hung on to the gusset with one hand and in the other hand I felt Gene's activity being telegraphed up his hose to me. I told Al that Gene's hose felt free. Then Al said Gene wanted me to start coming up on his hose. I wedged myself tight into the vertex and sort of straddled the gusset plate. Both hands were now free and I began pulling up Gene's hose. In this intermediate hose pulling position I had the responsibility of making sure the topside crew is picking the slack up from me at the same time and speed that I am pulling it from Gene. If there is a difference, some loose excess hose might get hung up somewhere. I had to make sure I kept the hose equally taut between me and the barge. We had pulled up maybe 20 feet of hose when Al said, "All stop. Now he needs slack. Slack him off."

This was bad news. It meant his hose had fetched up tight around or under something. And he needed slack to clear it. I started pulling his hose back down from the barge and paying it down to Gene. It was hard to pull. Then I noticed that the tide was turning and starting to press our hoses against all the braces. Damn! Things were getting more urgent.

After a few minutes Al said, "Hold that, hold that. All stop." I stopped and waited. Then Al said, "Gene's all clear. He's coming up. Pull him up to you." I began pulling. He was coming up fast. I told Gene's tender, "You've got to take up slack faster". The next thing I knew he was right alongside me. His hose was pulled out of my hands and then he was up and gone. I didn't know what he was using for a down line. Was he using my hose or had he found the cable going to the top of the leg?

I stayed wedged into the crotch for a bit longer. Then Al announced Gene was on the surface and for me to get ready and come out. Well, I crawled out of the crotch and groped around. I either found the cable or a line or something. I just can't remember what I used, but I went up and over that top brace and to the surface. I hadn't been down deep enough or long enough to require decompression, so I came right out. Al took off my helmet, removed my weight belt and said Gene was fine and already at his chamber stop. There were relieved smiles on the deck. I walked over to the chamber and looked into the port at him. We both kind of grinned and nodded.

Those first two days diving the Inlet on Platform Baker had a tremendous impact on me. I had done a variety of commercial diving jobs in California, however the Cook Inlet was a hugely higher level of diving challenges. Thinking about these challenges inspired some extreme adjectives: demanding, adventurous, scary, thrilling and powerfully satisfying! Those two days set me on the course of becoming a lifelong Inlet diver.

The sixteen platforms in Cook Inlet are places of adventure for their divers. But the fact is that these platforms all differ from each other. The diver adventure is different for each one. This reality makes it challenging to try and present pictorial information for each of them. I have chosen a few platforms that give a good basic representation. From there, I will discuss the variations on other platforms.

Jiggs, Owen and Gene

CHAPTER 2---THE GRAYLING CATASTROPHE

The Grayling under tow.

Most platforms were towed to the Inlet horizontally and afloat on two platform legs. Flotation was also provided by the huge air tight structural platform braces. Using a system of valves, all braces could be flooded with sea water in a controlled way that would cause the platform to slowly change from a horizontal to a vertical orientation. In April, 1967, the platform Grayling was towed into the upper Inlet. My diving partner, Jack O'Brien and I, had been specifically hired by the Graylings' Project Manager to assist in this process of getting the platform ready for the final installation on the sea floor.

The rough ocean journey to Alaska required that a pontoon, filled with air, be temporarily welded securely to the bottom two legs of the platform to aid in flotation for this massive structure. At the end of each leg was an attaching mechanism of huge hooks, one hook on the pontoon, one hook on the leg, hooked together before the trip began. As long as the platform remained horizontal the hooks stayed engaged. There were two plates welded to each leg to ensure that the pontoon remained firmly in the hooks during the voyage to the Inlet. Our job was to sever the plates. After Jack and I cut the plates, the plan was the hooks would remain mated, only unhooking when the platform would begin its planned vertical descent. Cutting plates off a pontoon was a tricky and sometime dangerous business as our experiences cutting plates off platform Baker had shown us. We couldn't help but wonder what the Grayling had in store for us.

The Grayling was already tied up to the derrick barge when Jack and I arrived. We set up our dive station near the end of each leg where all our hoses could be coiled. In addition to each diver's air supply/communication hose, we had a torch hose for each diver and an oxygen hose taped alongside a long electrical welding cable. Two men tended these hoses for us-paying them out or retrieving them as needed. Our dive radios would be monitored by another tender, Bill McWilliams, back on the derrick barge.

Jack and I decided to burn the two plates off one leg at a time. He would take a plate on one side of the leg and I would take the plate on the other side. We would burn them in half simultaneously. That way we would both be prepared for the final severing. Jack dove down to check out the two pontoon hooks we were relying on to remain mated together. There was one on each leg. Both big hooks were properly mated-up in the platform's leg huge pad-eyes alright, but he wasn't impressed by the structures intended to hold them up.

Jack came back up, and we started cutting plates. It took about 90 minutes. We made sure we were synchronized and then made the final cuts. The plates severed apart instantly and violently, shaking the leg heavily and accompanied by a short-lived sound of shrieking metal! This was a daunting and scary experience.

We got out of the water, the tenders took our helmets and weight belts. We sat quietly and thoughtfully at the barge dive station for a while. We looked over at some small diameter vertical pipes sticking up out of the water from the top of the pontoon. Their position looked about the same as it was before we performed our dramatic surgery. That was reassuring, but the noise and violence of the separation rang alarm bells for both of us.

The Grayling pontoon was held down, completely submerged, with about two feet of water over the top. In previous years I had seen other pontoons this size floating freely and almost completely out of the water with only a small section submerged. This revealed the tremendous entrapped buoyancy power locked in the Grayling pontoon. When all four safety plates were cut, those two hooks and their support braces, were supposed to hold against a horrific upward buoyant force!

What Jack and I were looking at was actually a monster that was supposed to be held in restraint by two lonely sets of hooks. We looked around at all the men working on the braces. They were clambering all over the structure. There were even men working on the upper leg, 65 feet above the water. Divers were also there, working on half submerged braces. We began a serious discussion about the possibility of the pontoon completely tearing itself loose from the legs when we made the final cuts.

Good commercial divers, especially Inlet divers, make an analysis and assessment of every dive. Not only what are apparent existing hazards, but what are the potential hazards if certain possible bad things happen. Procedures must be devised to deal with devilish possibilities. With all that in mind, Jack and I created a scenario to deal with a torn-away pontoon.

We decided that all workers must be completely off the platform at our plate cutting time and moved on to the derrick barge. This would include all shallow water divers, as well as the riggers on top of the legs. No one was to be on the platform except for Jack and me and one tender who would be in a good flotation full length dive suit. We would coil extra lengths of our diving hoses on the dive station. Extra lengths of torch hoses will also be coiled down. We also had recently tied a long one inch diameter nylon retrieving line onto the pontoon. That too would be coiled. It would be up to

Jack and me and our tender to make sure all hoses were leading fair and clear of any structural hang-ups before we began cutting.

Jack and I went to see the project manager. We described the dramatic violent reaction to our plate cutting. Jack also mentioned that he had gone down before cutting to examine the hooks. He felt that the H-beam supports should have been bigger and more rugged. The project manager was definitely concerned. He asked what we thought about all this. We told him we had work procedures we believed would keep everybody safe, even if the pontoon broke loose and the platform legs plunged to the bottom.

We spent a half hour discussing everything with him. We emphasized how important we believed it was to get every person off the platform when we made our cuts. Finally, he agreed. He said he liked our scenario and would make sure the other divers were off shift when we dove. We decided to dive the next day on the early, high slack tide, and then went out to begin to transfer all our gear to the end of the second leg.

The next morning we began as planned. As before, our dive radios were on the derrick barge, tended by Bill McWilliams. Jack and my hoses were both tended by Mel Mellin at the end of the leg. He had intercom communication with Bill. Jack and I visualized where our safe positions would be. We started the dive by checking that each other's hose was indeed free and clear of the platform.

Finally we were satisfied and we started our cuts. We never got to the ends of the plates. What remained of the uncut plates suddenly began ripping apart and tearing away- hooks and all. A horrible, hellish sound! The pontoon ripped up and away in a roaring cascade of water. It was like being next to a volcanic eruption! I later learned the violence of this was transmitted to the upper end of the platform.

In all this wild turbulence, the lower ends of the platform legs began a 50 foot plunge to the sea floor. I found myself being dragged down head first…very bad for a heavy gear diver. All the air in the helmet and suit will go to the legs. If not remedied quickly, the diver will be blown up to the surface upside down. I pulled my knees up to my chest and went into a head down crouch as the lower platform legs hit the sea floor. I waited in my tight crouch for whatever was going to happen next…..but nothing. There was a sudden stillness.

Slowly and warily, I stood up to deal with my problems. My weight belt shoulder straps were coming off. One was gone and the other was heading that way. Weight belts are worn loose and shoulder straps are vital. If I lost my weight belt it would drop off, the air in the suit would go to the legs and the probability was that I would be blown up to the surface upside down. While I worked getting one strap back over my shoulder, I realized I was fouled in two different places. Bill McWilliams, sounding stressed and worried called, "Owen, are you OK?" I was worried too, but I tried to reassure him. "Yeah, I'm OK, just fouled in a couple of lines. How are Mel and Jack?"

"We just got Mel out of the water and they are trying to get Jack out now."

After the pontoon busted loose, the lower 2 legs crashed to the seafloor.

In contrast to the ominous quiet surrounding me, I could hear pandemonium up on deck: the sounds of men shouting and yelling coming over the dive radio. All this time I was struggling to get my weight belt back on securely and the two fouling lines off me. One line was a cable of some kind and the other was a soft rope line.

Suddenly my air supply dropped….fast. I said something to Bill like, "My air"…..but then I couldn't continue speaking. A premonition overtook me that I might not get out of this one and that I might not see my wife and children again.

An odd calmness came over me and then I heard and felt a snapping sensation. With a shock I found myself watching that struggling diver. He was about 8 feet away. The black zero visibility Inlet was transformed into crystal clear water. I could see the diver clearly with a bright light illuminating him. I could see how the lines had him fouled and prevented the weight belt straps from getting back on properly. I paid close attention to all these things I saw him doing.

Suddenly, my air supply began returning and I abruptly snapped back into myself. Bill called, "Owen, Owen! They just got Jack out onto a raft, but they didn't tell me that they had to cut his hose to do it. Then I knew why you'd lost your air. I just closed the valve to Jack's hose. Are you and your air OK now?"

Both of our air supply valves were on the same tank. When they cut Jack's hose, all the air in our tank vented out the end of his hose. Then I asked him how Jack was. He told me something had hit Jack's helmet putting a big dent in it that banged up his nose pretty good. Other than that he was fine. What a relief. It would take more than a whack on the nose to slow down that good tough Irishman. I was still astonished at everything that had happened to me but I pulled myself together and told him I was OK.

The tide had turned now and was beginning to accelerate. I had to get these damn lines off and secure my weight belt. Then I remembered my "vision" and how it showed the lines encumbering me. Holy Hell! Sure enough! I felt them and recognized the lay-out I had "seen." The "vision" had not been just a wild hallucination. The complexity of how I was fouled was difficult to evaluate in the black moving water. I suddenly realized that the "vision" was a clear picture of how I was fouled.

The cable was my torch hose welding cable and the soft line was the nylon rope we had tied to the pontoon. It also had a half a wrap around me. That line was tight and had the cable trapped. It probably started pulling on me when the pontoon pulled up and away. I pulled out my knife and cut the rope. Then I yanked both ends free from me. This enabled me to pull the cable loose and cast it off. I then lifted each weight belt shoulder strap into place over the breastplate and began following my diving hose, coiling it in my hand as I went.

I followed it all the way back to where our diving station had been. There was not much slack left in the hose, but I knew I had enough to get to the surface. Thank goodness we had coiled all that extra hose. I closed my helmet's exhaust valve and opened up the air control valve. My suit quickly began inflating and up I went. I payed out hose as I ascended. It's called a controlled "blow up." I tell you I was grateful when I reached the surface. I adjusted my valves to neutral and looked around. A barge anchor cable was in the water near me and I grabbed it. I told Bill where I was. He sounded so relieved. What a horrible morning it had been for all of us.

While I was hanging on to the cable I looked around and was amazed by all the boats. Some were zooming around on some seemingly important mission. Others appeared to be on stand-by, waiting orders. While I was watching the nautical congestion, I saw a light gear diver with swim fins on swimming towards me on the surface. He seemed to be pulling a long line from the derrick barge. As soon as he arrived at my side he went to work tying that line securely around me. I was grateful for the immediate help he gave me.

Bill later told me the diver was Pete Blommers, the owner of the Calif. Diving company working on all the brace flanges. Pete stayed right with me while a towboat with a raft alongside edged over to me and helped me up onto the raft. The tide had turned and was starting to run hard. They pulled up the remaining slack in my air hose and then cut it in half. This made me wince a little but I was grateful to be rid of it.

The towboat returned me to the barge. I shook Pete's hand and thanked him. It had not been an easy task to come and help me.

An accident of this magnitude could have easily killed people. Some had to be taken to the hospital but amazingly there were no serious injuries. Blommer's diving crew was off shift, but the riggers and welders had been left on the platform to continue hooking-up brace flooding hoses, contrary to what the Project Manager/Superintendent had agreed with us to do. Some accounts said eight men had been flung into the water, other accounts said twelve.

At least they had life preservers on and stayed afloat until one of the many boats got to them. That's what all those boats were doing when I broke surface and looked around. The lives of all these men would never have been endangered if they had not been allowed to work on the platform while we were diving, as Jack and I had requested and the Project Manager/Superintendent had agreed to but hadn't done.

Jack and I went looking for him. We were informed he had to go to an upper level, important meeting. He was gone, but I never forgot the callous decision that endangered the lives of so many men. Perhaps we were lucky we didn't find him.

CHAPTER 3---BURNING OFF BAKER'S PONTOONS

Baker had been towed to Alaska on its side on two legs like a catamaran. The legs and their braces didn't provide enough flotation, so a long 10ft. diameter pontoon about 100 feet long was sistered alongside each leg and welded to it by two sets of wide, one inch thick plates.

When the platform had been righted and set into position on the sea floor, the pontoons had to be severed from the legs. Gene and I were given that job. We were both known to be very successful "burners." That means a diver who can use an underwater cutting torch to cut a thick steel plate in half. Even in clear water, "burning" is a difficult skill and Inlet divers must do it in zero visibility water.

Before the cut begins, an electrical grounding lead must first be attached to the work. An oxygen hose is attached to the torch handle and a welding lead also. A fitting on the head of the torch holds the hollow 14 inch long insulated mild steel burning rod. A trigger on the torch handle controls the flow of oxygen into the rod. When the diver is ready to cut, he makes sure the surface oxygen tank valve is open and that the regulator is set at 100 or 150 psi. He squeezes the oxygen trigger to check that there is good pressure coming out of the rod. Then he puts the rod tip to the cut starting point and tells his tender to "Make it hot." The tender will close the knife blade switch, sending 400 DC amps down to the tip of the rod, and the diver squeeze the oxygen trigger. At the tip of the rod the metal is melted and blown away. A hole is created.

In 1978 the BROCO cutting rod was patented and soon totally replaced the old mild steel rod. It uses oxygen in the same manner, but only needs a maximum of 150 DC amps. The secret materials in the BROCO rod create a temperature of 10,000 degree F. at the rod tip! It can cut through concrete as well as metal. It can cut thin metal just by "dragging" it with the tip aimed backwards. However, best of all, divers have found that it works wonderfully well in the conventional manner previously described. The cuts are even made more easily and quickly. What a wonderful invention.

But this was 1965 and the old style cutting gear worked very well for Gene and me. We met with the Barge Master, the job supervisor, and the job engineer who opened up a blueprint and discussed it with us. The horizontal one inch thick plates were a little more complex than we were originally told. There was one at an upper level and another at a lower level. They were roughly seven feet long and fit tightly between the curvatures of the leg and the caisson. But each horizontal plate had two vertical gusset plates between the leg and pontoon. The cut would have to connect to the cut in the horizontal plate. That added a little complexity, but was easily do-able.

Then all three of them looked a bit uncomfortable as they informed us that the cranc would not be available to hold the pontoon for the final cut! What the hell! Gene and I looked at each other. It is accepted practice in the construction world for a sizeable object to be hooked up and held by a crane when the final severing cut is made.

Most commercial divers would agree that "burning" is probably the most dangerous thing that we do. It's not the risk of a torch explosion. It's the risk of the big heavy object you've just cut loose, breaking the restraining rigging and lashing back at you. Even a well rigged object can rotate and lurch around when the final cut is made.

The three company men had the good grace to be embarrassed and apologetic. They explained they were behind schedule in getting the pilings into the legs and that they had to have all 32 of them stabbed and piledriven well over 100 feet into the sea floor by the time ice came into the Inlet.

All these deeply driven pilings provide the platform with the strength/stability to endure the winter battering of acres of three foot thick ice pans ramming into them at 6 knots. There were eight piling holes in each leg. Each hole required five or six pile sections to be stabbed and welded together on top of each other. The bosses said they wanted us to leave a small amount of metal uncut, just enough to keep the pontoon from toppling over until a tow boat could get to it and pull it over and away. Well, Hell! Gene and I debated that one awhile. Where was the good breakover spot? How much metal should we leave? We finally made a "by the seat of multiple pants" decision and went to work burning.

Unfortunately, the shortest crane swinging route to the piling stabbing holes was right over the pontoon we were cutting. Swinging a crane load over the heads of the crew has been a riggers code "No, no" for many years. We requested that they swing around from the other direction while we were diving. It would take a little longer, but for goodness sake, it was only for an hour at dive time three times a day.

They honored our request for the first dive, but not the second. Al Wickman, my tender, went over to reason with the tough Cajun foreman. He didn't seem to like Alaskans or divers and was giving the crane signals that swung the pile right over our heads. He did the same thing again on the third dive. Gene and I were both in the water, but Jim Dominish, Gene's tender, witnessed everything that happened from that point on.

Al was a man of action with an explosive temper and things were gonna happen. He headed for that foreman fast and with clenched fists, when he spotted "Big Boy" Thomasi, the Barge Master. Hell, even better. Big Boy was probably 6 foot 8" and 300 pounds of formidable looking man. He was also pure Cajun. He enjoyed playing the Cajun card game of Bourre after shift and so did Al. Al was smart and witty and Big Boy took a liking to him.

Al turned from the foreman and headed for Big Boy at a dead run. He leaped up on Big Boy's back and grabbed him by the neck and shoulder. Jim said Big Boy didn't even flinch. He just looked a little sideways at Al and said: "Al, whuffo you do that?" Al had calmed down a little and he explained to Big Boy, "whuffo". The pilings were never swung over our heads again.

Big Boy liked our diving crew. Gene and I were in the barge radio room with him one day when he got a call from the master of the barge's big tow boat, the Evelyn Edwards. The boat had gone on a mission to a local port, and had gotten a combined cable and rope badly fouled into one of the propellers. They hired a local diver to unfoul it but the diver said it was such a bad mess that the boat would have to be hauled out on the shipyard ways. Big Boy told the captain to bring the boat back to the barge on the one good engine. "We've got DIVERS over here. They fix it," he said. He put a very complimentary emphasis on the word divers. Made our chest puff out a little. It <u>was</u> a mess, but we cleared the propeller in two tides.

With the issue of swinging the crane over our heads settled, Gene and I decided we would burn the bottom plate first and leave 5 inches uncut on each of the two vertical gussets. We would save the top plate for last and make a total complete cut on it. That way we could get out fast with a quicker/shorter escape route if it started to go over. We could both dive the shallower plate, but when we approached the final severing cut, one diver would exit before it was made. We flipped a coin to choose who (looking back at our careers, I think Gene and I flipped a coin quite a few times). I won. Gene made the final cut and exited safely. The pontoon remained upright and the tug boat was summoned.

The boat crew rigged it and payed-out about 100 feet of pulling wire before starting a gentle pull. The pontoon eased over into the water at an angle and then the whole thing suddenly popped to the surface and floated serenely. How could we have had any misgivings? The deck was lined with appreciative observers. Gene and I tried to be modest in our acknowledgement of all the congratulations.

A tug boat immediately began moving anchors so that the barge could be properly positioned to work on the last pontoon. We decided to duplicate our last procedure. The second pontoon plates were identical to the first ones. After completing the cuts we stood on deck watching the tug boat hook-up exactly as before. The tug boat took the slack out of the pull line and began a gentle pull. The top of the pontoon moved a little bit, but stopped. The boat pulled harder. No change. This time the boat put a strong steady tension on the pulling line and kept increasing it until it was obvious to all that the pontoon was not free. What had happened?

Gene and I were stunned. Our friend, the Cajun foreman, rolled his eyes upwards and then just shook his head. We looked questioningly at each other. Then the questions. Did we get both gussets cut? Yes. How about the two 5 foot lengths of uncut metal? They were left exactly as the first one. We both knew that our cuts had been good. But there was no alternative. We had to retrace our cuts, and we did. We finished our retracements and came out. There was no question. Our original cuts had all been good. The boat was right there and took a pull. It still would not move.

Both Gene and I knew the answer. There had to be a third plate that wasn't shown on the blueprint. There was still some dive time left. I jumped in and went to the lower cut plate. From there, I slowly descended, feeling the pontoon and the leg carefully. About

10 or 15 feet below our lower cut plate, I ran into two vertical plates welding each side of the pontoon to the leg. They were about 4 feet high and one inch thick. As soon as I got out of the water, Gene and I went to the project engineer's office. We were still in our diving gear. He was properly embarrassed. The plates I had found were not on the blueprint, but he had found an E.O. (engineering order) to install the plates....written in pencil no less.

Well, it was nice to be vindicated but now we're really in a dilemma. Should we still rely on the uncut four inches on each side of the lower plate and completely cut the two bottom verticals? Or should we finish the two 5 inch cuts on the lower plate and leave some metal on the bottom verticals. Leaving two 5 inch lengths of uncut metal worked very well on the first cut and it might have worked in our present predicament except, perhaps, for one important difference.

We did a great original cut, as proved by the easy removal of that first pontoon. However, we must confess that even great burners like Gene and me (ahem) leave a few missed spots here and there. However, the first pontoon pull-over by the tug showed that we left no significant hang-ups. But, going over all our cuts again guaranteed that all normal little rough areas were no longer there.

We double checked our second cut. We dragged our rubber gloved fingers over every little inch. It was a long, continuous pristine, open spaced gap! Would the two 5 inch lengths of uncut metal still hold against such perfect severings? We hoped so! We decided to completely cut the bottom and leave the two 5 inch uncut metal remain that way. We knew that both plates could be completely cut in one dive by two divers, but it would be dumb to cut them both simultaneously. Two dives would be made. The first dive would cut the first plate. The second cut would cut the last, dangerous one.

Out came the old coin toss. Lucky Gene not only completed the first cut but also got some of the one I would do. He also got the down line rigged right to the job for me. It's important for a burner to have some sort of line to stand on or hang one arm over. The cut went real well. Vertical cuts often go smoothly. I had about 4 or 5 inches left to cut, when Gene got on my radio.

"Owen!" he yelled. "The pontoon is starting to move. We can see it move up here. Don't press your luck. Get out!" Get out now!" "Up on the torch!" I said and it went flying to the surface. I was already on the down-line.

"Up on the diver." I said and up I went. I got on the decompression weight line by the dive ladder, so I missed out on what happened next. Gene said that about 10 minutes after I got on the weight line, the pontoon started over and just kept on going for a minute until the "uncuts" broke and it blew to the surface. The tug boat soon arrived to take charge of our recalcitrant pontoon. Ultimately, the engineers had done us a favor, because we learned to always ask if there were any E.O.s they might have forgotten to tell us about. And, also, next time leave a longer length of metal uncut.

CHAPTER 4---Getting Sid Out

In 1971 Gene Cleary formed his own diving company and I went to work for him. In August 1974, the Cleary diving crew went to platform Baker to install cathodic protection anode sleds. Unusually strong, naturally occurring electrolysis threatens all Inlet platforms with severe corrosion. Engineers combat it by setting an array of anode sleds around most platforms and one or two under the center of each platform. The sleds contain a large hunk of superconductive metal that is about 2 by 4 by 8 feet in size. The weight varies between 12,000 and 16,000 pounds.

Each sled is connected to a platform D.C. generator by a very heavy duty electrical cable which is pulled up the platform J-tube. A J-tube is simply a pipe that goes down inside a platform leg and curves to exit through the side of the leg. It is welded to the leg and usually extends 12 to 18 inches out from the leg. The anode is electrically charged in a manner that causes the electrolysis to eat the anode metal instead of the platform.

To set anodes around the platform, the process goes like this: the end of a strong pulling wire is sent down from the platform and out the J-tube and on to the sea floor. The diver takes down a winch wire from the boat and shackles it on to the pulling cable. His job is done for now. The J-tube cable is pulled to the surface. It is shackled on to the end of the anode cable which is then pulled up the J-tube. When all the allowable sled cable has been pulled up the J-tube, the boat will then set the anode into its proper location on the sea floor.

To get an anode sled under the center of the Baker Platform, it is first necessary to pull its connecting anode cable down through a triangle formed by the platform's top braces and an identical triangle formed by the bottom braces, which would give it a straight lead to the J-tube. (see drawing) My job was to take a guide wire through the top triangle and then down through the bottom triangle. Then I was to deliver the end of it to Sid at the J-tube. He would shackle it on to the end of the strong pulling cable coming out of the J-tube. The end of that cable was then hauled back up through the two triangles to the surface for use on the boat that was setting the new anode and cable.

The sled setting A-frame boat was moored over the top triangle. Crewmen carefully tended the cable as it was pulled off the deck of the boat and down into the J-tube. When the cable pull neared completion, the sled was carefully lowered down through the

GETTING SID OUT

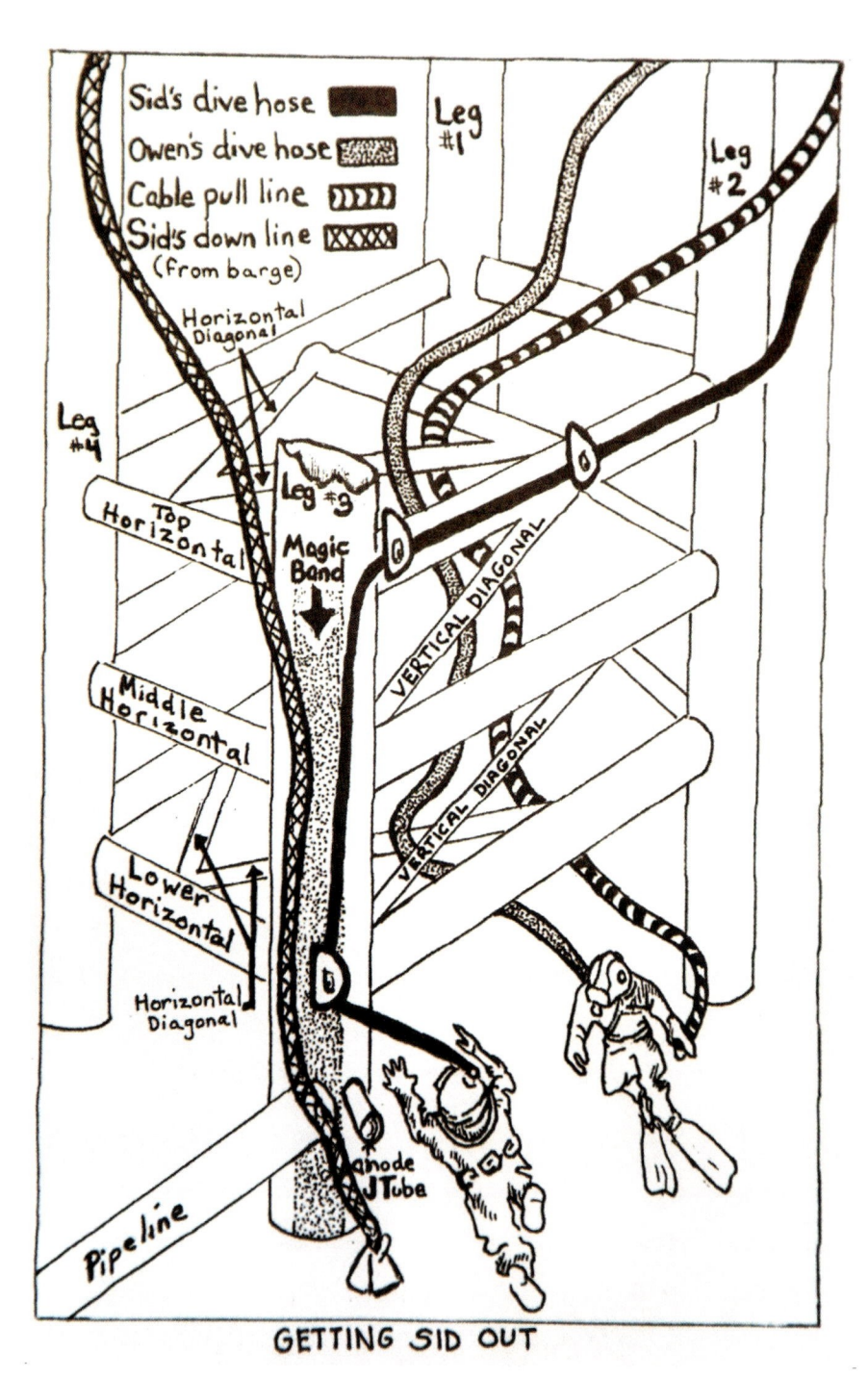

42

two triangles to its proper position on the sea floor. The diver would unshackle the sled and inspect the cable lay----- if the tide allowed.

"Swimming the braces" to run the guide line was a demanding dive....perhaps even challenging. The oil company requested that we do this on the next tide. This was a high tide just coming off a minus low, but still quite decent. Highs are much better diving tides than lows at Baker. Sounded good to me!

Unfortunately, it turned out to be too good to be true. The oil company supply boat had suddenly become available. Now the oil company bosses wanted to spend the next tide transferring all our gear onto it and get the present boat off the payroll, but, worst of all, even knowing the difficulties of the upcoming dive, the oil company bosses, wanted my guide line dive to be done on the following low tide. Something about "the schedule must be maintained."

Especially on the east side of the platform, low tides start veering to the south west as they slow down and begin to become divable. They never stop though, and when they achieve a westerly direction they start accelerating back to the north and become the start of the flooding high tide. Diving the platform's east side on a low is asking for diving hose hang-ups.

Despite knowing the danger attending low tides, the oil company supervisors still wanted it done on the low. The second diver, Sid Jirik, was to be sent down ahead of time to wait for me where the 4 foot horizontal joins leg 3 and the J-tube. He would take the guide line I took down and hook it up to the winch wire coming out of the J-tube and I would pull myself up the guide line and get out.

I studied the platform blueprints and decided that the fastest way was to dive down the big braces on the inside of the platform, but outside of the 2 -1/2 footers. I could still follow the guide line up and out, but stay clear of the 2 -1/2 foot vertices where the braces join with their hose hang-up gussets.

The boat was tied up alongside legs 2 and 3 with the bow facing north into the tide. Then a line on a 70 pound drill bit was lowered alongside leg 3 to be the downline for the J-tube diver, Sid. I liked diving partners with Sid. He was a great partner: strong, super-competent and dependable. His Czechoslovakian accent took a little getting used to, but it was worth it. He was fun and a classic old time heavy gear diver. No Sir! None of that fancy new-fangled gear for him.

Bill Biller, the deck diving supervisor, told me he was going to be right by my radio all the time. That was good to hear. He knew what we were up against. Bill was an experienced Inlet diver. In fact, we'd dived partners on a Baker job a few years previously.

I got all my gear on and went to the side of the boat. A weighted cross-over-line had been thrown from the boat over the top of the horizontal brace running between legs 2 and 3. I jumped in and followed the cross- over- line to the brace. I had the nylon cable pull line with me. I searched along the interior of the horizontal, and soon found the 2-1/2 ft. horizontal diagonal joining it.

The braces led and connected up to a 2- 1/2 ft. diameter brace running perpendicularly in the center of the platform between the east and west seven foot diameter horizontals. (see drawing.) All three of these braces were mated together.

Then I pulled the cable pull line down inside the triangle formed in the center of the platform. Taking the pull line with me, I followed the platform's east face vertical diagonals down to the sea floor. The 4ft. diameter horizontal brace was only about 6 feet off bottom. I walked along the bottom feeling the braces overhead and I quickly found the lower triangle. I stabbed the pull line down inside it and brought it out underneath the horizontal brace.

Then I noticed that the tide was changing direction from southwest to west. It was also accelerating and it was getting harder for me to maintain my position. If the current had washed me around to the side of the leg, it would have carried me irrevocably downstream away from the leg. I asked Bill if Sid had gotten to the J-tube area yet. He told me Sid was near the bottom, but was having trouble getting slack in his hose.

"Bill, how does the tide look?" I asked. I knew it had changed direction to the southwest down here. How was the tide running up there?

"The tide is starting to turn southwest, but velocity is still about the same," he said.

"What's Sid's situation now?" I asked.

"He's gotten to the leg but he still can't get around to the J-tube," he answered.

"Bill, this sounds bad. Can you pull up any of his hose?" "We'll try," he answered. He sounded worried. I waited. "No, he's hung up real bad, he answered." Now he sounded alarmed.

"Bill, I'm going to finish running this line through the lower triangle and secure it and get back up to the surface, so I can see where his hose goes." "Tight line my guide line and also my hose." I noticed that the tide was going west now, and velocity was increasing. Oh Damn! "Up on the diver," I said. The line was snug and I had no trouble following it.

As soon as I reached the surface, the tenders pulled me over to Sid's hose. They pulled our hoses close together and I grabbed it. Sid's hose led horizontally to leg 3 in about 20 feet of water. It was hung up behind a burned-off turning cable pad-eye shackle. I pulled it free. "Tight line his hose," I called out. It fetched up tight, still horizontal, but further around the side of the leg. I followed it. Double Damn! Hung up behind another cable pad-eye! I pulled it off the pad-eye and the shackle. Finally I thought hopefully, it's free. "Tight-line his hose," I called out again. His tender tight-lined his hose, but it still wasn't free. It was bar-tight and heading directly around the leg.

I pulled myself over to the south side of the leg. Oh Hell! The tide had turned completely to the north and pinned me against the leg. I knew how strong the tide was running down there where Sid was and it was fast working its way up to me. A sort of wild desperation overcame me. How was I going to get Sid out? How was I going to get back?

Bill's voice cut through my turmoil. "Owen, Sid knows what you're up against. He said to tell you that it seems impossible to him for you to be able to get down there. If you agree, he wants you to tell him so that he can start cutting his hose and drop his weights. He wants to try coming up free."

This was a death sentence! No sir! That wasn't going to happen. I was shocked into cold hard thinking. Nowadays, most divers wear an emergency air supply bottle, but then, Sid would have had to breathe the air inside his suit and helmet. Perhaps the air would last for 7 or 8 minutes at that depth. If he did manage to free himself completely, he would have to ascend his down line, fighting a terrible fast current while he was possibly losing consciousness. I had to go down and try to help him. The current was really pinning me against the leg now but I could still move around…..and suddenly the answer came to me.

This narrow vertical band of water pinning me against the leg was perhaps a little more than a foot wide. The current quickly started washing out around the sides of the leg at each side of the vertical band. I realized this current could be our way out. Sid's hose was staying within this band as it went down the leg. At this advanced stage of the tide turn, the water velocity would continue to increase……but it would also maintain its present northern direction.

My decision was immediate. I realized I could use the

"magic band" current to keep pinned against the leg while I pulled myself down his hose! I told Bill I needed tenders on the radio so they could react fast when I needed them to adjust our hoses.

Bill let Sid know I was coming. I pulled myself hand over hand down Sid's hose. Believe me, I was concentrating all of my being on this descent. A light side pull told me I was beginning to fall around to the inside of the platform. "Tighten Sid's hose," I requested and I was quickly pulled back to the center line of the "magic band." I pulled myself down slowly and carefully with the crew on the boat making hose adjustments so I could stay within the "magic band".

I guessed I was more than half way down the leg and Sid's hose was still going straight down.....Suddenly I knew where it was going. I had been up and down this leg many times over the years. The only thing I knew of that could trap his hose like this was a big pad-eye welded on the leg just above the pipeline coming out of the leg. I kept going down and there it was! I also ran into Sid's down line. I told Bill what I had found and to get somebody to tend Sid's down line. I took a pull on Sid's hose just downstream of the pad-eye. His hose felt free! I could feel him move.

The pad-eye was just about at the current center line. I thought that it might help hold me in place while I pulled Sid around the leg to his down line. I told all this to Bill and had him tell Sid to get ready. Bill relayed and Sid replied he was ready. I told Bill I would yell "GO" and let's do it. I yelled "GO" and was startled how fast Sid got around the leg to me. He must have been really scrambling while I was pulling. I gave him the down line and up he went. I was right behind him. We really scrambled up that line. We had to fight the current to get to the ladder. The tenders hustled us into the recompression chamber, helped us out of our gear and closed us into the inner lock.

    We just sat silently for a while and then Sid looked over at me and very quietly said, "Thanks, Owen." I was touched and embarrassed. All I could think of to do was give his baseball cap a little tap and say, "You would have done the same for me." His Czechoslovakian emphatic reply was, "I vould haf tried." And I know damn well that he "vould haf".

    After we got out of the chamber, the boat's captain invited us up to his quarters. He didn't say much. Just had us sit down and poured us each a glass of whiskey…which we gladly grabbed.

    Sid retired a few years later and began making sheath knives. He gave me one. It reminded me of him…tough, rugged, and would hold an edge for a long time.

    Twelve years after our dive he got stomach cancer. I went to visit him in the hospital. I was truly shocked at the deterioration of this once strong, vital man. But he stood up and we walked to the window and looked out while we talked. A little cot had been set up crossways at the bottom of his bed for his wife, Shirley, to sleep on.

    Sid died a week later. Soon afterwards, Shirley invited me to come over and view all of his diving gear. He told her I was to look it over and take anything I wanted. Well, damn, he had made a good looking rugged weight belt, and I also took some of his fine diving woolies. We were the same size. Farewell, Sid.

CHAPTER 5---HAZARDOUS ADVENTURES

Many new platforms were installed in the late 1960's. This was an especially adventurous time for Inlet divers. A brand new platform presents the diving team with the challenges of the unknown. Each platform has its own tide action characteristics that can only be learned the hard way – in them. The platform blueprints and engineering orders must be studied by everyone. It's a scary adrenalin pump for the whole crew when a diver gets his hose hung-up around a strange pipe-stub nobody knew was down there. The diver's hose must always be checked well before the tide turns.

Pipes protruding out of the side of platform legs are the main hazard for the diver's hose. They can be at various elevations on the legs and usually extend out about 18 inches from the leg. The end often has a bolted flange. These pipes are often water intake suction tubes and very dangerous. I know a diver who got sucked onto one. He had to cut a piece out of his dive suit to escape! We quickly learned to have the platform people shut off any water suction near our work site.

In my experience, the most dangerous things on a new platform are the "temporary construction assisting devices" that have been installed but not remembered. You've got to ask knowledgeable platform people about them. What are they, where they are and how many were installed? Unfortunately, such knowledge is hard to find. Some workmen probably had no idea they were creating a booby trap for divers. Others intended to remove the menacing hardware, but that was probably sabotaged by the last minute rush to get that platform on the bottom.

The Osprey

On the Osprey platform we quickly discovered that the construction crews had left numerous six inch angle irons welded onto all the legs- and widely distributed. There was no predicting where in the hell they would show up. We spent a lot of time in the early dives pulling our hoses off them. We decided that the only way to deal with them was with two divers in the water. One diver would tend the hose of the working diver from an underwater location offering a good safe hose lead. This worked very well. We also needed another diver to standby for the two in the water.

This is a good example of the unknown dangers awaiting the divers on a new and unexplored platform. There were a lot of these menacing discoveries made on new platforms in every era. We dove the Osprey in 2001 and 2002, still finding unremoved, temporary construction hazards.

The Dolly Varden

In 1967, Jack O'Brien made a dive on the newly installed Dolly Varden platform. I was a diver on the second shift. Jack's job was to find a pipeline J-tube coming out near the bottom of the northwest leg, inspect it, and tie a down-line around it. Jack got to the bottom, all right, but when he reached bottom he realized his hose was fouled somewhere above him.

The platform installation crew had run water hoses over the braces to valves that fed water into the braces. This was the way all floating horizontal platforms were transferred to a vertical position, and an eventual descent to the sea floor. To provide a run-way for the hoses the crew had laid long lengths of chain-link fencing over the braces. The platform started heading down before they could get the fencing removed.

During the descent, much of the fence came loose and formed a terrible chain-link entanglement. Jack found that his hose had been snared in that horrible entrapment mess! He tried desperately to free his hose, but it was hopelessly fouled. Gus Clemens, the standby diver on deck, heard Jack's description of how badly his hose was entangled. He grabbed a big bolt cutter while the tenders quickly put on his weight belt and helmet. Then he descended down Jack's hose. He followed the hose to the entrapment and started cutting the fence wires. Gus finally got Jack's hose free, but was dismayed to realize that his own hose was now enmeshed in the snarl. Jack grabbed the bolt cutter and began cutting the chain links away from Gus's hose.

A crewman ran down the stairs into our bunkroom. He yelled at us to get up and get our gear on. We might have to go down and help them. We raced up the stairs and got our diving gear on as fast as we could. While we geared up we listened to the dive radios. It was immediately apparent how dangerous the situation was. Jack had freed Gus's hose, but his own hose had become re-ensnared. The tide had started to turn. Things were becoming desperate. I grabbed a bolt cutter. I was ready to go when they told me they both had gotten their hoses free. Up they came. What a relief!

Spooling Up

A few years later, a new platform was put into commission. Two pipelines had been laid and were ready to be connected to the appropriate J-Tube on each of two legs. This process is called "spooling up". Before it could be started, blank plates had to be unbolted and removed from the flange at the end of each J-Tube. The blanks were bolted on to protect the flange from damage during the long sea voyage to Alaska. A circular ring gasket was installed between the blank and the face of the flange. This effectively prevented sea water from filling the tube. However, it created the necessity of completely filling the tubes with water to equalize the inside/outside pressure on the blank and free it up for removal. I got the removal job.

We called the platform and asked them to fill the J-Tubes with the pressure equalizing water. They replied they had already done this.

I took down a heavy hammer and a big pry bar to put into the gap between the bolt hole rings on the blank and the bolt hole rings on the flange. The gap is created by the circular flat face of the flange that juts out from the area inside of the bolt holes. Sometimes blanks had to be pried off because enough counter-balancing water had not been pumped into the J-Tube. I took the bolts out of the first one and beat it with the hammer. Nope. Still stuck. I got my big pry bar into the gap between the two sets of bolt holes. I braced myself and heaved. It suddenly came off, and a strong water flow rushed into the tube.

"Hmmm, they didn't put enough water down the tubes. Well, anyway, it did finally come off," I thought to myself. I moved over to the J-Tube on the other leg. Same deal. The hammer wouldn't budge it. I put the bar between the bolt rings and braced myself even more solidly than I had done on the first one. I gave a mighty heave…

Holy Hell broke loose! Instantly my left arm was completely sucked up into the J-Tube and my shoulder was wedged tightly in the mouth of the tube. My large heavy gear breast plate was pulled hard against the flange. I was trapped! The suction force was so powerful that I couldn't push or pull myself free. This sudden violence wrenched a wild yell out of me--- startling my tender. "What's wrong?" he yelled. I told him and urged him to call the platform fast and have them pump water into the J-Tube double quick. I was sure the tube was nearly empty. It would fill and equalize eventually, but my breast plate had the end of the tube pretty well blocked. I had to get out of there before the tide turned!

I kept on struggling to free myself. Finally, about ten minutes later, I managed to pull my arm out of the tube. My left hand was bleeding and a couple of fingers were broken. This earned me a ride on the helicopter for a trip to the hospital. I ended up with the tip of my index finger skewed noticeably to left. The third finger has a permanent 45 degree angle at the first joint. There's also a bit of mobility discomfort, but essentially, the hand works as well as it ever did. However, I'm glad I'm not a pianist or a violinist. I'm a trombone player, and all is well in that arena.

The Adventure of the 5th Leg

In May 1966, Derrick Barge 7 had the job of picking up and stabbing a 5th platform leg through a big circular ring welded out from Baker's northeast leg. The size of this ring required two divers, one on each side of the ring. The stabbing guide was placed 30 feet underwater. Another, smaller derrick barge, the 250, was tied alongside us. Their job was to pick the foot of the leg when Derrick Barge 7 had picked the top of the leg well up off the deck. The leg was huge.....10 foot diameter, 160 feet long and 150 tons!

Gene and I were gearing up in the "Round House," on the Derrick Barge which was a strongly built room under the supporting foundation of the crane, which was now revving up. We looked outside and saw that the crane had the top of the leg high up in the air. Barge 290 was beginning to pick the foot. We resumed dressing-in when there was a huge, powerful thudding crash. The deck plates shuddered. We ran back to the door and looked outside.

It was a riveting scene. The picking point at the top of the leg had failed. As the leg hurtled to the deck it threw a sudden surging load on to the smaller crane. This tore the crane boom completely off the 290 and sent it plunging to the bottom of the Inlet. The leg bounced once or twice onto a large open deck section of our barge and it started to roll towards our side of the barge! The only thing between this monster and the side of the barge was big Bob Rasmussen. He knew he was fleeing for his life. The sight of his big size 15 boots flailing the deck is etched in my memory. Gene and I opened the door wide and jumped out of the way to let Bob plunge in…Rolling thunder went right by our refuge and then over the side it went. Quiet.

Big Boy Thomasi was the derrick barge superintendent. He and his foreman made a fast checkup on people and equipment. Miraculously, no one even had a scratch. Our barge was totally functional. Big Boy completed his assessment. He came over to us and said in his very strong Cajun accent: "I'd like you two divers to head on down there, now, and hook onto that thing so we can pick it out." Gene and I digested his words for a silent moment. This big guy's calm confidence was so impressive that my first thought was, well, sure, Big Boy, Uh, yeah, whatever you say. You bet.

And we did "head on down there." We reached bottom at 120 feet and put a down line on the leg. We also ran a messenger/pulling line underneath. Unfortunately, the leg was sitting on a big gravel bed and was in line with the current direction. It settled down into the gravel bed and was half filled with gravel in two days! We got help from two more divers. In about three or four days we had a picking wire rigged at each end to form a big bridle. The pick was made. One of the big wires broke. By now the leg was full of gravel. The added weight was just too much.

They decided to leave it and build a new one. Years later a diver was setting an anode sled near Baker's northeast leg. He informed topside that he had found the top of a big long pipe. I happened to be topside listening to the radio and I happily informed him about the dramatic history of the pipe. He was impressed.

A Hazardous Adventure of a Different Kind

Somehow bars, beer and divers have always found each other. I've been in a few after long and thirsty diving jobs, but my favorite bar has been the famed Hunger Hut at home in Nikiski, AK. The fact that the Hunger Hut is at the end of a long walk uphill from the dock, toting bags of gear, might have enhanced its allure. Smoke filled, built like it was thrown together in a weekend, it was a welcome haven for an Inlet diving crew. It had the rep of being a tough bar.

One memorable occasion happened after a long, hard job in the inlet, long before there were cell phones. We finally finished the job one afternoon, and went to the Hunger Hut where there was a public phone. We called the women in our lives to pick us up. While we waited, we sat down at the bar side by side, and discussed the job over our drinks. Two of the best tenders in the Union, Al

Wickman and Henry Napier had been on this job with us. Al sat on my right and Henry sat on my left. Al was strong, smart and annoyingly mouthy. Henry was small but wiry and usually a thoughtful speaker. Both tenders took good care of their divers, but often had strongly opposing ideas for getting a job done.

They hated each other.

We settled in for the usual re-hash of the job and looking over the growing group of patrons. It was getting to be cocktail time at the Hunger Hut. The noise level began to rise as the bar seats were soon all occupied – many of them by women. It was fast becoming a noisy party and you had to be loud to be heard over the hubbub. Henry was still talking to the guy next to him. At this point, I realized he was saying loud and extremely insulting things about Al! Both Al and I heard him. Al jumped off his bar stool and faced Henry.

'Are you bad-mouthing me you no-good-son of a bitch?" Al roared, starting to lunge at Henry with murder in his eyes. I had seen Al in action before. I knew Henry was in real peril. I didn't even take time to think. I had to do something to save Henry. I jumped in front of Al, face to face, chest to chest. I threw a quick, powerful tight bear hug around him, trapping his arms to his sides and clasped my hands tightly together behind him.

I yelled, "Run, Henry, run!"

Al struggled to free himself. He was strong but so was I. We staggered about, still tightly clasped together. We fell to the

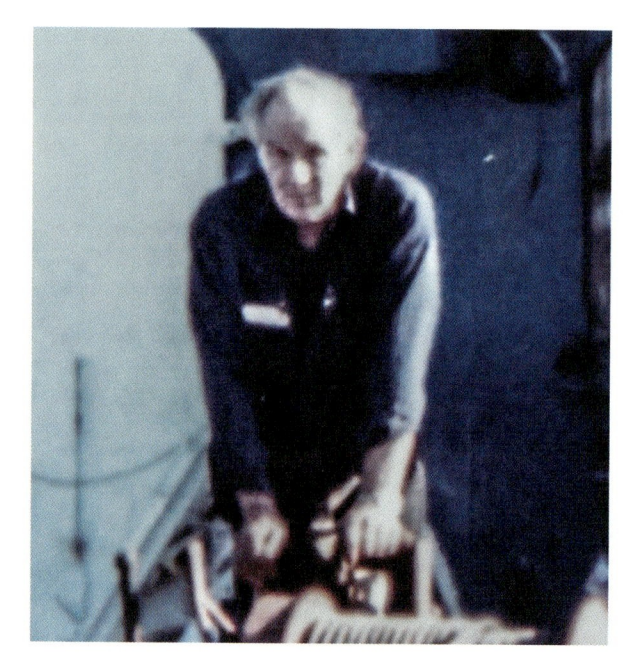

Henry Napier

Al Wickman

floor but I kept him pinned. Two of the crew threw themselves down on top of us to help me keep Al trapped. By this time, I was flat on my back which gave me a panoramic view of the bar. The expressions of the people on the bar stools ranged from serious concern to laughter. One woman had a fearful look on her face and put her hand to her mouth. Another was laughing hysterically. The rest of the men saw this as an appealing sporting event, and they piled on top of us. When somebody yelled that Henry was safely gone, we disentangled ourselves and stood up.

Al wasn't hurt and forgave me for saving Henry, so we went back to drinking until our wives showed up.

Crane delivering crewmembers to the Shamrock.

CHAPTER 6---ICE

Slots created in the ice when it crashes through the platform legs.

In the winter time, the total upper Inlet is menaced by huge, thick, dangerously propelled ice pans. Between late November and early April, sheets of ice are created that are often more than 1000 feet across. Records over many years pretty much agree that the average ice thickness is 3 feet, but it can get up to 3-1/2 feet thick. Two feet of the ice pack floats under water. The visible top foot is often a dirty looking grey in color.

The ice packs are quickly and easily propelled by the Inlet currents and tremendous force is applied to anything that gets in their way! I have been on platforms that have been rammed by these most formidable creations. Even if you believe you are in a safe place, it is still a fearsome experience. A power contest will ensue. The ice may finally start cracking open where it bears against the legs. In a strong current, the ice may grudgingly begin a slow steady crumbling that will allow the pan to slowly and haltingly proceed downstream.

Open water slot-like openings will appear and lengthen in the ice, as it pushes it way through the legs. The open water slots will be almost exactly the width of the legs. Fifteen or sixteen feet! There are groaning/growling sounds, as the ice grinds laboriously along. Even though the ice is moving, it is still wedged tightly against the leg. The legs are buffeted and they shudder. Walking becomes unsteady. Coffee is sloshed out of the cups. Trying to get a good night's sleep is a challenging experience. When the ice finally breaks free and continues its journey, the slots will remain visible. It is an impressive sight.

The Inlet platforms are built to resist the onslaught of the thick moving pans of ice. The legs of each platform are supported by the pilings driven down inside them. Most platforms have eight cylindrical piling in each leg. Most of them are between at least 2-1/2 ft. and 3 ft. in diameter and least 1 inch thick. As pile driving commences, additional sections are welded on to create a continuous piling that penetrates between 100 and 200 feet deep into the sea floor. Each platform is different. The pilings are stabbed through a series of strong rings that are secured to the leg and well structured. Platform Steelhead is the largest platform in the Inlet, and is in the deepest water...200 feet deep. Steelhead has 12 piling in each of its legs. Most other platforms have eight.

Upper Inlet ice is so powerful and dangerous. First of all, Inlet ice weighs 64 pounds a cubic foot. That's the weight of sea water. Every square foot of the top of an Inlet ice pack represents containment beneath it of 3 cubic feet of ice that measures one foot square by 3 feet deep, and it weighs about 192 pounds. A 200 foot square ice pan would have an incredible weight of four thousand tons: 200 feet by 200 feet equal 40,000 square feet. Each square foot has 192 pounds beneath it that adds up to about 8 million pounds, or 4000 tons. And Inlet tides push it around seemingly effortlessly.

There is another aspect of this called "Impulse Momentum," which states: the force exerted by a moving object against a stationary one is directly proportional to the velocity of the moving object. An ice pack ramming a platform in a two knot current would hit it twice as hard as it would have in a one knot current. A large ice pan ramming a platform in a 6 knot current is dreadful to contemplate -----but it has happened many times.

Ice flows will often ram a platform at an angle instead of squarely. Perhaps it will only hit one leg and use that leg as a fulcrum to rotate around to the side of the platform. It will then continue its downstream journey, and probably just go down alongside the upstream fulcrum leg and downstream leg below it.

But there is another potential danger. A platform crane is usually located midway between the two legs. Supply boats come alongside the platform to send up supplies and equipment. In the short daylight wintertime, this mission often has to be done in the dark. Platform lights illuminate only the immediate vicinity. The ships' spotlight only illuminates a short distance and ships' radars are incapable of detecting ice flows. It is surprising how quickly an ice flow appears out of the upstream darkness and threatens a boat alongside the platform.

In 1966 the bolted flange ends of two delivery pipelines were connected to Platform Baker. The end of each pipeline was bolted-up to the short bolted flange tube sticking out near the bottom of a designated oil delivery leg—two pipelines, two legs.

The winter of 1966/67 was a cold one. There had been a lot of ice ramming platform Baker ---huge pans of it. In later years, many other platforms were installed higher up in the Inlet. They helped Baker by breaking the huge pans into less forceful smaller ones. But in the winter of 1966/67 the lonely Baker had earned the well-deserved nickname of "Old Shaky." The engineers also began detecting slight pressure losses in the two pipelines. They immediately suspected that the shaking legs had caused the pipeline connective flange bolts to loosen a bit.

Platform Baker's supervising engineers asked us to put a complete diving station on their supply boat. The supply boat would be on stand-by as close to the platform as the ice would allow. In

Supply boat plowing through the ice to get to the platform.

the meantime, we would live on the platform. This was the quickest way to make a bolt-tightening dive if an ice-free interval suddenly occurred.

It was not unusual for diving to be done from a supply boat. This one was big, about 160 feet long, fast, and had good twin-engine maneuverability. There was plenty of deck space to accommodate all of our diving equipment and not interfere at all with normal supply boat operations. On board living accommodations were limited, but the platform took care of that.

Some supply boats had doubler plates welded onto the entire bow area to help protect against bow-butting ice. Damage occurred anyway. Rudders and propellers, as well as hulls, have suffered ice damage. Worst of all, ice has crash/crunched more than one boat down onto the sea floor!

Experiencing the unrelenting ice pack attacks on Baker was like living a James Bond adventure. I've already described ice slot creation. The other fascinating adventure was watching the supply boats using the platform crane to off-load supplies and equipment. I admired their skill and bravery. They had to clear out fast, when an ice pack nosed out of the dark towards their boat. But, one night, things just went against them. They were in the middle of hooking up a huge compressor to the crane. It required big rigging. The sea was a bit rough, too. Three boat crewmen were on top of the compressor. One man was trying to hold the crane cable steady. The other two maneuvered the big shackle in the end eye of the crane cable over to the "picking eye ring" atop the compressor. The shackle pin was almost tight when a huge ice pan came out of the dark and hit the upstream platform leg. It immediately began to pivot.

It was a large ice sheet that extended well out past the leg. It used the leg as a fulcrum, and rotated down-stream and around towards the boat. It was going to act as a wedge, squeezing the boat under the platform! Around it came and fast. The skipper had no choice. He had to back out of there now. On the radio and by loud speaker, he told the crane operator to pay out slack and told the crew to try and unshackle the compressor while he backed out!

The ice came hard against the side of the boat and started squeezing it towards the middle of the platform. The three crewmen were desperately trying to unshackle the sling, while the crane operator kept paying-out slack. I could see him clearly. He was standing up in the cab, leaning forward toward the window to gain as much visibility as he could. The crane wire was at an angle of about 45 degrees, when I heard a yell come up from the boat. A crew man had fallen off the top of the compressor as they had finally pulled the compressor free! The other two men jumped off the compressor and went to the aid of their fallen comrade. I could see that he had been hurt, in some way. We later learned that he had broken his arm. That was an adventure those men and I will never forget!

Years later, an almost identical incident occurred off a different platform. The crew had almost finished shackling the platform crane load line onto a huge machine, when a fast moving ice floe came suddenly out of the dark. It hit the leg and pivoted quickly to threaten the boat. The captain had no choice. He had to back away fast. Unfortunately, this crane could not have had nearly as much cable on the drum as the one on Baker had. The water's tidal current added power to the boat's velocity. The cable surged tight with tremendous force. The boom was torn off the crane and was sent crashing down onto the ice! But, worst of all, the crane operator's control booth was built onto the base of the boom. He was also sent hurtling down onto the ice!

Platform in the ice. Compiled by Belmar Engineering, Redondo Beach, Ca. for the Cook Inlet Regional Citizens Advisory Board

The crew quickly adjusted the boat for a rescue mission. The captain brought it alongside the ice floe. Three men jumped onto the ice and ran over to the stricken crane operator. He was still alive. They gently extracted him from the control booth and worked out a procedure to carefully carry him to the boat. They had almost reached the boat when they realized he had just died in their arms.

The owner of the boat quickly assembled an emergency replacement crew. He knew how painful all this had been for the stricken men. He gave them all time off to go home and recover as best they could. A friend of mine was a member of the relief crew, and years later he still talked about it.

A tide-driven pack of ice, jammed-up motionless against platform legs, will often reduce the tremendous pressure by splitting into two sections. The broken-off upstream half will then start a life of its own. It will begin a process that is incredible and spectacular to watch. The broken-off upstream end will climb up on top of the motionless downstream half- and the whole intact upstream half will follow the lead! It will appear to easily slither along down the surface of the entire length of the downstream half-until it also jams to a stop against the two legs. Now there is a 6 foot high wall of ice pushing against the platform, but only about four or five feet is above water.

This process is called "rafting" by some Oceanographers, and can be very troublesome. Eight foot high rafting has been reported at Baker. Some of the pipes and hose extending below the platform were threatened. The extensive abrasion of ice packs on all platform legs has required that protective half-round doubler sheets be welded around the vulnerable leg areas. During that two week stay on Baker, I saw a lot of ice action.

I saw more rafting, slotting and ice pivotings around the legs. What a dramatic experience it was! The ice maintained a continual, relentless presence, so the company decided to delay the diving job until spring. I've always been so grateful I got to experience all of that almost "other worldly" winter life on platform Baker.

In 1967 our diving crew connected two oil delivery pipelines to the brand new Grayling Platform just as we had done on Platform Baker in 1966. The pressure test passed with flying colors just as it had on Baker. We were becoming famous for our flange-up tube jobs. However, the winter of 1967-1968 was another cold one and the battering ice flows were plentiful. Grayling had short flange tubes for pipeline connections near the bottom of two legs. It was quite similar to Baker and guess what? The battering started them leaking also. The engineers got our diving crew out there – with one big difference. Instead of living on the platform, we were to live on the platform's supply boat. This boat was at least 160 feet long. There was plenty of room on the deck for all our diving equipment including compressors and the big recompression chamber. The state rooms had to be reorganized, but they finally arranged accommodations for our six man crew. The boat was to stay clear of the platform until an ice free tide appeared. The engineers said that a helicopter would survey the platform area before dive time.

We had just finished getting the boat all rigged up for diving when we got the call to come to the platform. It was dark, black night, but the platform did appear ice free in the limited visibility area around the legs.

The head supervisor on this job was from the South, and totally unfamiliar with winter ice conditions in the Cook Inlet. He came to the boat to talk to the diving crew and the Captain of the boat. He told us that a helicopter had surveyed upstream and said they had seen no ice "nearby." (I was skeptical as I had hadn't heard any helicopters). But then he said he wanted the Captain to tie the boat broad-side to the current on the up-stream side of the legs, with the bow end tied to the upstream leg and the stern end tied to the other upstream leg! His reasoning was that if the ice did come down, the boat itself would prevent the ice from getting to the diver's hose! Then he quickly went back up on the platform. Even in the summertime, most captains would never tie a boat up to a platform in that manner.....even to the downstream legs, much less to the upstream legs.

Those early Inlet years were an especially dangerous time for divers. Many early bosses simply didn't comprehend what a dangerous place the Inlet is for divers. The more enlightened ones consulted with their divers to determine the most effective way to accomplish a job. I still remember them fondly. With others, however, it was a struggle. This flange tightening job was starting to have a scary feel to it.

The Captain was a good, experienced Inlet skipper. We talked this dangerous request over together. We both had seen frightening close calls with the Inlet ice. How powerful and quickly maneuverable it is. But we did agree that tying the boat to the legs would buy some escape time for a threatened diver.

The Captain maneuvered the boat gently and deftly against the legs, even though the tidal current was still running three knots against them. This was helpful for us, though. It gave us time to set-up for the dive. Inlet divers must wait to jump into the water until the current slows down to a little less than one knot.

When the boat was securely tied to the legs, the Captain turned on the powerful search light atop the wheel house. He aimed the beam on the water that was coming down at us out of the black night. Then he watched the water while we completed the pre-dive preparations. In about 30 minutes, the Skippers urgent voice boomed out over the wheelhouse bullhorn. "Quick! Cut the tie-up lines." We ran to the legs and saw a huge pan of ice bearing down on us. We got the lines cut free just as the ice whammed hard into the side of the boat. The Skipper gunned the engines....first forward and then in reverse.....but it was too late. The ice had jammed the boat tightly against the legs. We were unmovably pinned against them.

I stood at the side rail of the boat, watching the ice intently. The boat's long aft work deck was close to the water. A metal sheet was welded vertically along the side of the boat to keep water off the deck, and also to act as hand rail and it seemed to be less than four feet high.

I could see in the illuminated area. Upstream, half of the ice sheet started to break in half. It severed itself cleanly and quickly. The "rafting" process had begun. The complete edge of the upstream half climbed rapidly on top of the downstream half, beginning a steady, relentless advance toward the boat. It hit high on the side of the boat, but it didn't come to a complete stop! It kept up some kind of urgent motion. Then I saw that it was working itself up the side of the boat. Higher and higher it came, until it reached the top and started to tumble into the boat!

I watched incredulously. Long chunks of 3 foot ice started coming over the top of the hand rail and went crashing down onto the boat deck. Some came down right next to my feet. They were thick and heavy. Ice was now cascading aboard the whole length of the long work deck hand rail. The weight of all that ice soon started causing the boat to list…and it quickly became worse. The boat's heeling-over made it easier for the ice to advance. It was soon rampaging aboard.

The Captain was a true man of action. He alerted the platform. A rescue crew quickly came down to the lowest platform walkway. It was about 20 feet above the boat. Then he told the boat crew to set-up an extension ladder from the boat to the walkway. All the while, he was still vainly trying to free the boat. By now, the attacking ice had caused the boat to heel over almost to a 45 degree angle. The captain gave the order for everyone to abandon ship…..the whole boat crew, as well as the diving crew! He intended to stay on board alone and keep trying to free his ship.

I'll tell you there was immediate compliance. There were almost a dozen of us who scrambled up that ladder to the precious safety of the platform. The ship's cook was the last crewman left on board. He made sure the top of the ladder was untied and then pulled it down onto the boat! I don't remember that he said anything. I think he gave us a smile and a wave and then he headed for the front of the boat and the stairs to the wheelhouse. One of the boat crew said something like, "Well, He's gone to help his friend."

I thought about that for a second and then took stock of myself. When I got off that rickety ladder onto the firm walkway, I think I gasped. I took a big deep breath and let it all out. For a moment I relaxed, but then horrible thoughts hit me. I looked down at the stricken boat. The heeling over...down on the starboard (right) side...had gotten worse. The low side of the long aft deck was filled with ice and water. The boat looked ready to capsize. I felt guilty for having deserted the brave captain and the cook, but there sure as hell nothing I could do to help them. I believe that all of us on that catwalk probably felt the same way.

We all crowded along the end of the platform catwalk to watch the heroic captain fight to free his vessel from the merciless ice. Forward and reverse, again and again. Up on the catwalk, we watched transfixed. Suddenly, the boat made some slight movement. The boat seemed to edge forward a bit...yes! The damn ice pack was shifting very slowly away from the bow leg. Now he was emphasizing the forward motion. Maybe back a little, and forward hard. The boat finally broke free and away!

There were no more attempts to tighten pipeline flanges that winter. In the ice-free ice springtime our diving crew accomplished the task and both pipelines passed the pressure test.

I was not personally involved in the following events, but I talked with people who had been, including some eye witnesses of the sinking of the Monarch. This is another account of the great dangers ice creates for the platform supply boats. It was January 15, 2009, early in the dark Alaskan morning, the 166 foot long supply vessel, Monarch, was in the upper Cook Inlet next to the Granite point platform. The Skipper was maneuvering the boat close to the legs in order to get under the platform's crane.

Suddenly, out of the dark up-stream, a big pack of ice came at them. The tide was still running pretty fast. The ice slammed hard against the boat and jammed it up tight against two platform legs. The Skipper tried forward and reverse at full throttle. The boat would not move. He immediately realized their terrible jeopardy. At about 6:00 AM he made a "Mayday" call to the Coast Guard.

Later I talked to a Monarch crewman who said the ice took over the vessel from the stern. It pinned it up against the legs of the platform and then just started to collect on the deck of the boat. Ice may well have been invading the boat over the stern, but the whole crew was startled at how rapidly ice and water were coming on deck, causing the boat to begin steadily heeling over. I feel sure that the ice pack performed at least one "rafting" maneuver that pushed ice over the rail and into the boat.

By now, the crew had undoubtedly donned their water proof flotation suits. There was no doubt but that the boat had started to capsize. The Monarch stayed afloat, but began a slow, steady rollover. The crew managed to scramble around on top of whatever part of the rolling over boat was still out of the water. The boat finally completed a 180 degree capsize. The bottom of the bow area was facing the sky and well out of the water and was holding steady in that orientation. All seven men had positioned themselves on this upside-down bow section.

Observers noticed that the boat was starting to sink stern first. However, the bottom of the bow section remained steadily upright and out of the water. It had also become noticeably more stable. Some observers thought this was because the stern may have settled securely onto the sea floor. The geometry could easily have allowed this to happen. The boat was 166 feet long, and the water at the platform was only 86 feet deep at that tide time. The fact remains, though, that this upside-down floating bow section provided the last remaining refuge for the seven beset crewmen of the Monarch.

Luckily, ice was still pushing the boat against the platform. The upside-down bow of the boat was directly under a platform catwalk. Somehow, the men of the platform provided the means for the men of the Monarch to escape their sinking death trap. There were no serious injuries. Around noon, the boat finally sank down out of sight. It was still in the same location.......alongside the Granite Point platform.

When inspection dives were made on the Monarch, the divers found the Monarch on the bottom, upside down and 6 to 10 feet away from the platform leg. The inspection revealed the good news that no damage had been done to the platform or pipelines. The divers were given the job of stabbing surface controlled suction hoses into all the oil and diesel fuel tanks to pump them out.

In June, a supply boat was chartered for this mission, but it proved to be too large and unwieldy. It was replaced by a smaller and more suitable vessel. The diving suction pumping program started in mid-July and finished in mid-August. A U.S. Coast Guard press release said that the divers had recovered 12,445 gallons of diesel fuel from the Monarch. The dives were described as difficult and risky. I can sure believe that! During the fuel removal process the divers discovered that two fuel tanks had been ruptured and seemed empty.

Multiple sonar inspections from January through August showed that the sunken Monarch had not moved. A divers' inspection said the boat was firmly embedded in the sea floor and had done no damage to the platform or the two pipelines. The wise decision was made: leave well enough alone. It seems ironic though. The Monarch's final resting place was next to one of the platforms it had serviced so dependably for so many years.

Diver checking the ice conditions.
Photo supplied by American Marine

CHAPTER 7---WODECO II

On October 26, 1966, my dive partner, Jiggs Jackson and I dove on a small drill ship, the WODECO II. It was the smallest drill ship that ever ventured into the Inlet and it was in trouble. What the trouble was, we didn't know, but we were there to fix it. What we did know was that we were the second crew of divers to be hired.

Jiggs drew the first dive. His job was to assess the damage. As he began his descent, he was immediately appalled. In order to begin drilling, the previous dive crew had tried to stab the flange at the bottom of the long cylindrical control stack, called the marine riser, onto the well head's baseplate flange. The baseplate was firmly anchored into the sea floor. For some reason, the bottom of the marine riser had surged around and struck the baseplate. The blow destroyed the hydraulic flanges' mating clamp, located on the bottom of the marine riser.

All of an unknown number of hydraulic hoses, descending from fittings at the top of the riser were freely blowing about…..before they connected to the bottom of the riser. This was like diving blind through a virtual writhing, snake pit of hoses making quite the challenge for Jiggs to wend his way through. He felt around the riser stack and discovered that hooks had been welded onto it in a staggered fashion. The WODECO crew had tried to secure the hydraulic hoses against the riser stack by running a line back and forth between the hooks.

Jiggs finally threaded his way through the hoses to the bottom. He felt his way around the base flange area and found broken pieces of the hydraulic clamp. He stuffed all the broken pieces into his chafing pant's pockets and began his laborious ascent, freeing his dive hose from the hooks on the stack up through all the hydraulic hoses.

Another diving hazard besides the tide blown hoses and the hooks snaring the diver's dive hose, was that the WODECO's anchors were inadequate, unable to hold the rig steady enough to allow the stabbing of the bottom of the marine riser flange onto the base plate flange.

The drilling supervisor sort of apologized to us, but said having to install "heavier" anchors had put them way behind schedule. Securing the hydraulic hoses in the usual safe way, (in a metal container chute) would just have been too time consuming. "We will bring the marine riser out of the water and tie the hoses back on the hooks with stronger line this time," he said. Also, he was going to completely remove the broken hydraulic flange connector. He wanted us to mate the flanges together with a standard, old Cameron clamp. It consists of two semicircular metallic pieces that enclose both flanges. When they are bolted-up tight together, the flanges are mated.

Jiggs and I unhappily digested all of that. First of all, the "heavier" anchors still weren't heavy enough. The drilling supervisor and I had been standing at the edge of the Moon Pool during Jigg's dive. The Moon Pool is an approximately 10 foot diameter circular opening to the sea in the middle of the ship. This is where drilling and diving occurs. We could see the constant one or two foot back and forth ship movement of the stack. We also knew that the bottom of the stack was moving in the same pattern. The repetitively changing angle of the taut baseplate guide wires verified that. Installing an old style bolted flange takes time. The flanges can't be moving around on you after you get them lined up and are trying to adjust and tighten the clamp around them. The wonderful advantage of the hydraulic clamp is speed, The instant the diver feels flanges line-up, he yells, "Close!" over the dive radio. The hydraulic operator listening to the radio responds immediately and the flanges are mated.

The WODECO II well head base plate on the bottom was standard. It had a six foot long vertical guide post sticking up at each of the baseplate's four corners where they were securely welded. These posts were geometrically located to stab into the four matching and slightly larger hollow stabbing guide pipes, projecting down from the bottom of the marine riser. (See photos)

In the course of more dives we did not even come close to being able to stab the flanges. The ship would just not hold steady. We would have them move the ship to the proper position, but it would slip away from it. Bring it back and it would keep drifting....even after all the anchor winches had stopped. There was too much slack in the anchor wires or we were dragging anchors...or both. Everyone on deck, watching the riser and guide wires coming out of the Moon Pool, could see all this as well as we could. We spent four days uselessly fighting all this.

Worst of all, the hydraulic hoses had all come loose again. When the hooks were no longer filled with hydraulic hose, they became the perfect entrapment for a diver's hose. The last dive was especially bad. I was heading for the bottom through a nightmare of hoses and hooks. I finally got near the bottom but my hose was caught and kept fast. It felt like it was snagged way high up. I dreaded having to claw my way back up there to clear it. I didn't have to. Jiggs got on the radio and told me to stay put. He could tell that I was hung up somewhere near the surface and he was going to down to pull my hose off the hook. And he did.

After he freed my hose, I decided to try and ambush the ship. I laid in wait as it drifted towards the flange at a steadily slower pace. Slower and slower. Hot Damn! I thought I might have lured it into a stabbing lull. Hell no! When it reached the flange, it just slowly veered sideways and reversed course. The tide started to turn a little. My tender, Mel Mellin, called me on the radio and told me it was time to leave bottom. Up I went and damn glad to do it, but I didn't get far. My hose was hung up…..firmly.

I pulled myself up to the snaring hook, coiling my hose in my hand as I traveled. Got it off! Okay! But no! Another hang up somewhere. I headed over towards it, but by now I had a big handful of my coiled hose to hold as firmly as possible while I was trying to snake my way through all those damned hydraulic hoses. Jiggs recognized my dilemma. "Owen, hang tight where you are.

I'll be there in a few minutes." I was still down pretty deep and I wondered how many more hooks above might have my hose. The tide turn was becoming stronger now. Jiggs wasted no time. He was quickly alongside me, helping me and himself get free of the hoses and the hooks.

We finally cleared our way up and out of the water. The tenders got our weight belts and helmets off. While they were removing our ankle weights and galoshes, Jiggs and I quickly reached a full and vehement agreement.

We'd had enough! We headed for the supervisor's office! We had not gone far, when we saw him hurrying over to us. Before we could say a word, he apologized profusely. He said he was completely shutting down the present operation until all the problems were fixed......and that he had already ordered major changes. He began describing some of them. We listened in surprised silence.

He said he was going to completely overhaul the anchor system. Some anchors would have a second anchor mated alongside. Other anchors would be moved to more effective locations. All slack would be tight lined out of every anchor wire. He said it would take a few days but they were going to work around the clock. He asked us to remain on board. We would be paid full wages until we could resume diving. Jiggs and I were in a state of restrained shock. We agreed to remain, even though we were wary.

Anchors that were earlier replaced by the bigger ones were still on board the big, anchor handling tow boat. Every working anchor had a strong picking cable buoyed off to it. The supervisor ordered the tow boat to pick some of the more crucial anchors and attach one of the smaller anchors right behind it. By watching the Moon Pool guide wires movements during our dives, the supervisor recognized the more movable/vulnerable areas. I think the anchors positioned to hold the ship against the direct flooding and ebbing currents were selected, as well as other crucial locations. He also moved some other anchors to more effective locations. All anchor wires were adjusted to remove any slack. He did exactly as he said he would.

While the anchor work was going on the crew was working on the marine riser. A new hydraulic flange clamp was installed on the bottom of the stack. A proper hydraulic hose retaining chute was also installed. Our nemesis hoses had been fettered. We were truly ready.

October 29, 1966. Jiggs and I flipped a coin. I won the dive. Yeah! The adrenalin enthusiasm started.

Connecting the marine riser to the base plate was scheduled for the midnight low tide. Lows slow down faster than the high tides and must be watched carefully. The crew had prepared the ship well. The marine riser had been pulled completely out of the water and extended way up inside the four legged derrick.

The stack was then carefully lowered down. There were distance measurements on the side of the stack. The rigging crew was careful to stop when there was about five or six feet between the bottom of the stabbing guide pipes and the tops of the well head base plate guide posts. The guide wires still looked vertical. The ships' crew had done wonderfully well. Now it was up to me.

I stood at the edge of the Moon Pool and took hold of one of the four guide wires. It was to be my guide to the flanges. When I got to the bottom, I located and assessed both sets of the four guide posts and riser pipes. Hot Damn! They were almost aligned! I felt the bottom of the riser. It was only about two feet above the tops of the baseplate posts. I could tell the marine riser was a little to the south of the base plate. All the anchor wires were ready to move. I immediately began instructions to the top side crew to stab the marine riser on the base plate.

"Have them come up a little bit on the north anchor. Real easy now." The top side crew then lined up the marine riser perfectly over the base plate. "Stop!" I called out.

Both sets of pipes felt directly lined up over each other. "Come down on the stack easy." I felt one of the stack stabbing funnels go over the top of its base plate pipe.

"All stop." I called out.

I checked all four sets of legs. They were all stabbed on. I crawled between the two base plates over to the flanges and made

Blow-out preventer stack

Base plate

sure the gasket was intact. It felt good. I moved out of the way and said "Lower the stack."

The stack was lowered until the flanges came together and the stack stopped descending.

I felt the flanges. They were tight together and lined up perfectly. I instructed topside to actuate the flange clamp and it worked!

"Up on the diver!" I climbed up the Moon Pool ladder and onto the deck. Mel took off my helmet. I was immediately greeted with smiles and congratulations. I knew it went really well but I didn't know how fast. Mel flashed an unusually big smile and showed me my dive sheet. The whole dive took less than 15 minutes. Jiggs clapped me on the back and said, "Great job." The supervisor came over and grinned when he said, "What took you so long?" The whole crew was elated. Everybody had done a wonderful job to make this happen.

During the dive, things were going so well that I was enabled to speed through the operation. The supervisor said they were starting the pressure test immediately. The goal was that it should hold steady at 1200 psi. In the meantime....sleep. (It took me a lot longer to write it down in this book than it took to do the job).

We came down to breakfast the next morning to greet more smiles. The pressure was holding good. They could start drilling and the dive crew could go home. Everyone was happy. Jiggs and I sure left that job with an entirely different outlook than the one we started with.

I remember most of this adventure without having to refer to my log book...but not everything. One thing I had forgotten was this: I had to work hard during that terrible dive with Jiggs to clear my hose off the hooks...during the descent as well as during the ascent. We left the job pleased we had stuck with it and that it had turned out so well.

CHAPTER 8---STEELHEAD

The Steelhead Platform was placed in Cook Inlet in early July, 1986. Right from the beginning this job became a monumental challenge for the divers. The Steelhead is located in deep water, about two miles west of the south end of Middle Ground Shoal. Seven miles to the south a prominent peninsula, West Foreland, juts out from the west side of the Inlet. This defines the location of an extreme narrowing of the northern Inlet ….and a strong increase of tidal velocities.

Other platforms are located near the Steelhead in water ranging from 100 to 150 feet deep each with their own diver/difficult tide action characteristics. The Steelhead, though, is in 200 feet of water. The tidal characteristics of Steelhead are probably the most diver/dangerous ones in the Inlet.

A particularly precise placement of the Steelhead was necessary. A barge was hired with 8 or 10 positioning anchors and a crane that could lift 2000 tons. The platform's legs and braces had been purposely flooded just enough to sink the platform in the water, but light enough so that the crane could perform any required repositioning.

The platform was held up off bottom by the crane, but it was also solidly secured against the bow of the barge. The position of the barge was moved by the barge's anchor winches. The barge movements were directed by the surveyors. When their instruments told them they had reached the specified location, the "Stop!" order

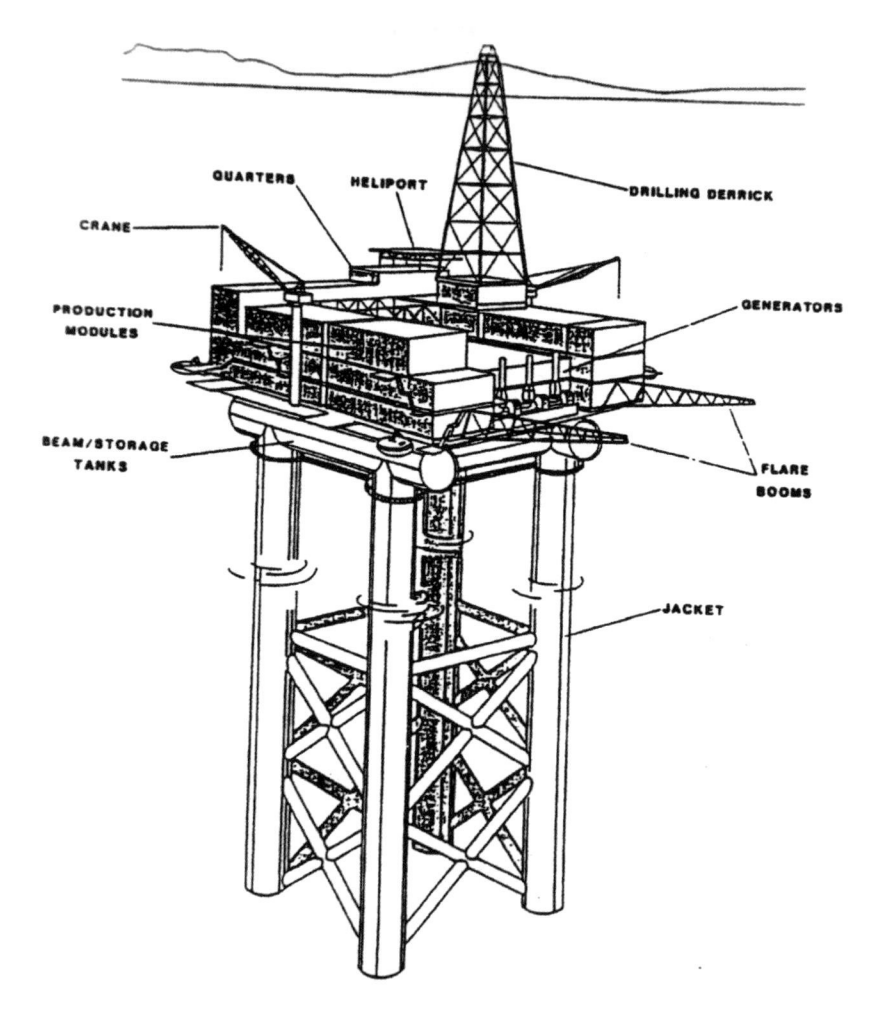

Isometric view of the Steelhead
Compiled by Belmar Engineering, Redondo Beach CA for the Cook Inlet Regional Citizens Advisory Council

was given. The crew removed the restraining lines and the platform was lowered to the sea floor. The surveyors made a final position verification check —and consternation ensued. The Steelhead was not quite where it was supposed to be.

The tide had turned and was starting to accelerate. There was no time to use the anchor winches. The superintendent ordered the crane to pick the platform off bottom and achieve the proper position by adjusting the crane boom position. Up off the bottom came the platform. Crane booms only have strength to hold a load that is hanging absolutely vertical. Any side hauls on the load can easily destroy the boom. The tidal current direction against the platform put a powerful "side-haul" on the boom---and it "exploded"! Witnesses said the boom broke into pieces with a roar! Much of the boom and the huge load-holding hook-and-block with all its pulleys and cables hurtled down into the center of the platform.

The WOTAN, a well rigged derrick barge, was brought out and anchored alongside the platform. A major repair and recovery program was begun. A company representative came on board to stay with us and get any sort of assistance we divers might need. He brought out a full set of platform blueprints. We studied the blueprints, I'll tell you.

Steelhead has some unusual characteristics. Many platforms have horizontal diagonal braces that crisscross the center of the platform to the brace on the far side. Steelhead only has braces on the far sides of the platform. All the vertical diagonal X-braces are 5 feet in diameter. The horizontal braces are 4 feet in diameter (see schematic). There are no braces at all going across the center of the platform. Numerous sacrificial anodes were welded on the top and bottom of all horizontal braces. We acquired a good blueprint of these anodes and saw how they were laid out on the braces. They were the most ultimate dive hose grabbers we had ever seen!

Each anode was about 6 inches square and about 6 feet long. They are welded to the braces by a short pipe about one foot back from each end of the anode. The two pipes are about 5 inches high. The 5 inch gap under the anode is perfect for trapping a diver's hose as he travels along the braces. There is about an 8 inch gap between anodes, but they are not all welded on the top of the brace centerline. They are staggered. One will be a little to the right of the centerline and the next one will be a little left of center.

In actual practice this makes them even more efficient hose trappers by the eight inch staggered gap between the ends of the anodes. If one doesn't snag your hose, the next one will! Each horizontal brace had eight anodes in line on the top and eight anodes on the bottom. These anodes look exactly like a long row of big ship mooring line tie-up cleats. There were some worried divers who readied themselves for this challenging salvage job.

Diving down into that chaos of the crane boom explosion was like descending into a huge endless spider web of two inch cables....many of which were fouled under the ends of anodes. The broken-off upper end of the boom was entangled in all the crane's cables. We realized we would have to pick the cables and boom out together, clearing cables out from anodes, as the WOTAN crane lifted them out. Some of the cables had to be cut in half with an underwater cutting torch. Other pieces of junk crane metal also had to be picked out. Numerous bent and torn-apart pieces of the boom were hung-up in the crane cables and anodes.

The crane boom wreckage only extended down to about 70 or 80 feet of water. The second set of horizontal braces was in about 102 feet of low tide water, so they sustained no damage. The top level of braces was in about 22 feet of water and sustained only moderate damage.

Some sacrificial anodes were mashed down flat onto their horizontal brace. Others had been torn completely loose from their brace. The cables from the crane hook/block were wedged under them and pulled them loose. Other anodes had simply disappeared. Some of the horizontal braces were damaged with long deep dents and abrasions. None were punctured, though. One of our salvage jobs was to take electronic water flooding readings of all affected braces. Fortunately, they were all still dry.

As we went about our salvaging tasks, the Inlet started educating us about the personality of Steelhead tides. Number one was the character of low tides. When the ebbing surface water had finally slowed down enough to dive, the water on the bottom had already turned and had begun flooding back in....fast! This strong change characteristic begins a steady vertical ascent to the surface.

A diver could be comfortably working away somewhere in mid-water when a flooding, rip current will slam into him with no warning and perhaps at a velocity between one and two knots! Obviously, this negative low tide personality trait completely prohibits diving the low tide on the bottom. We tried diving the lower horizontals down at 102 feet by trying to monitor the dangerous low tide reversal. We didn't have the wonderful sonar water velocity indicator in those days which can quickly reveal the water velocity at any specified depth. We put a weighted line a little over half way down and watched for the line to veer over at an angle when the current hit the weight. This proved to be adventurously undependable as stray rip currents could cause a false reading of the line!

After a lot of wrestling cables out from under anodes, we finally got all of the crane parts out of the platform. What a relief! It had only taken us one week to accomplish the salvage, but it sure seemed longer than that.

Diving from the WOTAN was very advantageous for us. There were plenty of sleeping quarters. It was scheduled to stay at the platform and assist with the construction. We ran two 12 hour shifts, each with two available dive times. The crews on each shift were mainly all divers. The water was deep and decompressions were long. At lot of dives required two divers and a standby diver. The depth meant there would be only one dive per man per shift. That's four divers right there. The others would have to be standby divers.

The six divers were me, Lief Simcox, Bill Morterude, Steve Stuart, Monty Mac Pherson and Mike Wheeler. We also had two

Bill Morterud and Leif Simcox. (B. Wick)

great tenders, Henry Napier and Eddie Mata. When the WOTAN left, we all transferred over to the Shamrock. What a superb, powerhouse crew! As the job progressed, I would occasionally be in a position to watch our wonderful crew in action. Sometimes the thought came to me: "This great crew could go anywhere in the world and excel." I still believe that.

The deep 200 feet of water dives would require 3 short in-water decompression stops at different depths, before the diver would come out of the water and get in the recompression chamber.

The diving crews were highly skilled at getting the diver out of the water, removing helmet and weight belts and getting the diver down to the proper depth in one of the two recompression chambers. All in less than five minutes! This is the magic procedure divers must follow to avoid the bends. After a deep dive and a lengthy decompression, the safe practice was to give the diver a twelve hour interval before his next dive. Extra divers were required. Two divers in the water creates extra challenges for the deck crew.

We began our very thorough platform inspection examining the sacrificial anode situation on the four top horizontal braces, located in about 22 feet of water at low tide. Our hose hang-up wariness of those anodes was soon verified—in spades. The first diver spent his whole diving time clearing his hose out from under the ends of anodes. It was quickly obvious that a second diver had to be down there in the water just to tend the traveling diver's hose. That's what we did and it was very successful. We also found it was valuable for him to tend the traveling diver's down line.

The enlightened oil company was glad to pay for anything that was mission enabling. The first diver has his own down-line, which he must be able to move, if necessary. The second diver must also have his own down-line. Each of these lines must have a rigger tending it. The two divers' radio tenders stand side-by-side with their dive radios in front of them. Questions and instructions from the divers must be passed back and forth between the radio tenders. It's a pretty tightly knit group, I'll tell you, but it works!

For the deeper horizontals in 102 feet we found it was best to have a hose tending diver remain at the upper level of braces at approximately 22 feet. This gave a helpful vertical as well as horizontal lead on the hose. We completed the upper braces inspection, and found more of the same kind of damage we had discovered during the salvage operation. In order to get down to the lower horizontals, we had to travel down the vertical diagonals. This turned out to be tricky. At this platform there was almost never a slack time. A water velocity slowdown never led to a complete stillness of water. Instead of going slack, the tide would simply start turning sideways. That was the preliminary step in turning completely around and accelerating in the reverse tidal direction.

The vertical diagonals are 5 feet in diameter and are mostly bare pipe. Their construction forms an "X". There are two of them on each side of the platform. One is above the other. There is one impressed current anode in the middle of each of the four components of the X and twelve of them on each leg.

In order to run the braces we found a wonderful secret aid! After a lot of experimenting we finally found some light portable horse shoe magnets that would hold the diver securely in place on the brace, even against a fairly strong current! We simply tied the horse shoe magnet on the end of the down-line and off we went. But the magnets weren't totally fool proof. Sudden rip currents occasionally came through that blew the diver right off the brace. His hose tender-diver on the upper brace would pull him up alongside and up to the surface they would both go. A low tide that has gone into a rapidly ascending fast flooding reverse has also blown more than one diver off the braces.

While we were inspecting the braces, the pile driver men had been hard at work. They kept welding on additional lengths of pipe until the 34 inch diameter piling had penetrated 135 feet down into the sea floor. The tremendous booming sound of the pile driving hammer is bad enough in the air but it is greatly magnified in the water! The big-hammer boys were considerate of us delicately eared divers and refrained from hammering during dive times. Interestingly, the divers were soon mobilized to aid them. When they finished the pile driving, problems appeared that only the divers could help them solve. It required diving down 200 feet to the bottom of the legs.

Steelhead dives to the bottom were only made during high tides. The first consideration for 200 foot dives was decompression. We followed the U.S. Navy surface decompression table using oxygen. We discovered that the Inlet almost always provided nearly exactly 15 minutes of divable water time at 200 feet. Occasionally, it was a little less. Only rarely was it any longer. There was a mandatory decompression schedule for 15 minutes at 200 feet in the Navy manual. It requires a 2 minute water stop at 50 feet, a 5 minute water stop at 40 feet and a 7 minute water stop at 30 feet. Then the diver rapidly exits the water and resumes decompression in the recompression chamber on deck. All within the crucial 5 minute on the surface time limit.

Unfortunately there were times when the tide change occurred so quickly and powerfully that the diver was prevented from getting all of the prescribed water stops. To avoid getting the bends, he was required to take Bends Treatment Table 5....a total of 137 minutes in the chamber. Any dive longer than 15 minutes required use of the 20 minute decompression table. I had more and longer water stops than the 15 minute table. If your dive lasted longer than 15 minutes, table 5 was your required pal.

The second problem was nitrogen narcosis. Around 175 feet the nitrogen pressure in the diver's compressed air starts acting like a narcotic. The diver has trouble concentrating and becomes confused more easily. The deeper you go, the worse it gets...and quickly. Each diver has his own tolerance to it. Most of us handled 200 feet competently. I would stop my descent briefly at 185 feet and check that all my tools were properly holstered, before heading to the bottom.

A new diver on the job got to the bottom of the leg and then started remarking how smooth and pretty the rocks were on that coal black sea floor. Holy Hell! I immediately told him to return to the down-line, but he liked it down there. I finally talked him into ascending the down line. He didn't achieve normalcy until he got to about 155 feet. He was a real good diver, though. We just kept him off the bottom.

Cook Inlet has a very high level of electrolysis and also contains contaminating dissolved chemicals and silt. The result is a metal corroding monster! Divers took metal thickness readings on the legs of many early platforms. The engineers were appalled by the metal thickness losses. Numerous large cathodic protection anode sleds were placed all around and under those platforms. A direct current is sent down a cable to activate the metals on these sleds. This is call an "impressed current." The Inlet eats the anode metal instead of the platform

Encircled walls of sand/cement bags were placed in the gaps between the platform leg bases and the sea floor. They prevented the fast moving corrosive water from attacking the exposed pilings. In retrospect, more than half of Steelhead's diving involved placing bags under and around the legs. Unsupported, off bottom pipelines also needed stabilizing. Any off bottom length of pipe over 40 feet long could cause weld breaking pipe vibrations. Divers would first stuff enough bags under the pipe to give it support. The bigger piles of bags were placed on top and around the sides. Divers are expert at immobilizing pipelines.

Sand/cement bag piles can range from small easily handled groups to huge piles of 300 bags, all tied together in a clump that looks like a rough 10 or 12 foot diameter sphere. When the platform crane picks up that monster pile and swings it over the side of the platform, crowds gather at the rail to watch the divers corral it. Later on I'll describe in detail how to accomplish the dangerous task of placing bag piles.

Other bottom tasks included hooking up cables for the pipe pulls up the legs J-tubes. The engineers also wanted platform electrolysis readings taken…mainly at crotches where the braces join. Some damaged braces had to be meter checked to see if they were flooded. It was also important that the inside of the legs remained dry with no sea water intrusion. To accomplish this, rubber seals encircled each piling where it went through its hole in the bottom of the leg. Sometimes those seals got torn away and sea water flooded the leg. Repairing those seals was the first job assigned to us.

Diving at the bottoms of legs was hazardous for the diver because his hose was frictioning against 200 feet of braces. When the tide turned, his hose could be friction-pinned so tightly against braces that the tenders could not pull him up. The standby diver would descend the down line with the fouled diver's hose in his hand. He would wedge himself as best he could, on or near the offending brace and help the tender pulling hose. This often worked, but not always. As a last resort, I had a short two-legged bridle for the rescuing diver to wear. It was on the end of a fast action winch wire. One leg of the bridle was secured to the rescuer's harness. The other leg would be secured to the stricken diver's harness. They would be pulled out together. In the 40 years that I can remember there were at least 4 or 5 such rescues, but there were undoubtedly others.

The normal Steelhead tidal actions were challenge enough, but there was something worse! There were maverick currents, independent of normal tides, and unpredictable. Oceanographers call them "rip currents," and say they can achieve velocities of 5 knots. I'd estimate the ones that hit us at Steelhead dive times to be about 2 knots. During normal high tide dives they could suddenly materialize, usually out of the northwest, and hit the platform at an angle that was almost designed to pin the diver's hose against the braces. These were the times that the bridle on the pulling wire could save the day and the diver! These were the challenges we faced when we went about doing our projects at the bottom of the legs. Checking the pilings coming out the holes in the bottom of a flooded leg was our first assignment.

The very act of stabbing a piling through a water-proofed hole can obviously cause damage to the rubber seal. The inevitable leaks have been dealt with over the years by pouring a heavy thick layer of concrete down a hose inside a leg to the bottom plates of the legs. This will usually seal off any leakage going out alongside the pilings. Three of the Steelhead's legs was sealed successfully that way. The fourth one, however, stayed stubbornly flooded. We divers were asked, "to crawl under the northwest leg and take a "look". There was a surprisingly big cavity under that leg. It may have been there originally, and current blasting around the leg may have scoured it out more. There was at least four feet of gap between the bottom of the leg and the sea floor.

The first diver to venture into that gap inspected every one of the 12 pilings. He found that six of them had concrete rings around the piling base where they entered the sea floor. Up above there was a gaping open slot around each pile where it came through the legs bottom plate. It was quickly decided that the best way to fix this was to drive a ring of wooden wedges into those slotted holes. That's what we did. It took us 13 dives.

After we had wedged-up all the obviously damaged six pile holes, we carefully examined the remaining six. They looked OK. There was just no place left to drive a wedge. On Saturday, Nov. 8th, 1986 we told the platform executives that the pilings looked pretty well caulked-up to us. On Sunday, Nov. 9th, the oil company people happily announced to us that they had pumped concrete and gotten a seal. Hooray! They praised our work and thanked us.

We had seen the four foot cavity under the northwest leg. Next we took a "look" at the southwest leg. Wow! It had a much bigger cavity. There was a good six or seven foot between the bottom of the leg and the sea floor. The two eastern legs had more modest two to three foot scoured cavities. We discussed these scours with the platform engineers. They wanted us to protect the pilings from the fast moving corrosive water. Their recommendation was that we completely fill the gaped under sides of the legs and the pilings with our sand/cement bags. Finally, a wall of bags was to be built up around the outside three or four feet of the lower end of each leg...a complete protective encirclement.

At this same time in mid-November 1986, the pipeline lay barge finished pulling the two pipelines up the south legs. We immediately began our inspection of them. There were long lengths of unsupported pipe. A lot of it was caused by the pipes being on top of widely spaced rocks or small hills. Perhaps we could remove some of the rocks. However, it was more likely that we would have to build supporting, stabilizing and immobilizing bag piles. I think we felt relieved that the 1986 dive season was over. That would give us time to ponder these challenges and devise the next course of action.

The 1987 Steelhead dive season was a stunner. The first thing the engineers wanted us to do was to stabilize the pipelines. The pipeline J-tubes were about 8 or 10 feet above the sea floor. This caused the pipes to stay off bottom for quite a distance until their arc of "unsupport" expired. Unfortunately, when they finally settled on the sea floor, it was not very hospitable. Besides the rocks and small hills, there were shallow trenches and many big holes...both under and alongside the pipes.

Fortunately for us divers, many of these culprits were within reach of the platform cranes. We, and that wonderful crane, placed numerous big bag piles into those cavities. Some holes next to the pipelines were four and five feet deep. One huge hole was 8 feet away from the pipeline. It required us, and the crane, to dump in five loads of 300 bags to fill it. Other loads of 250, 300 and 350 bags had to be placed. When we got out of crane range, the dive boat, Shamrock, was used to bag. The Shamrock had a wide low bow and a big adjustable A-frames. It could handle loads of 40 to 50 bags.

The most astonishing thing about all this is that it was done while "live boating," although sometimes we worked close enough to the platform to install helpful hang-off lines on it. However, the Shamrock's two engines did it all. The divers' very strong down line was the only rope going from the boat to the pipeline. The bag pile from the boat was messengered down this line.

The bag line would sag when the bags hit bottom. The captain worked to maintain his vertical down line position, but the bag line was slacked off a bit to prevent any dragging. This operation was done shortly before dive time. When the tide slowed to dive time, the diver grasped the down line/messenger line loosely in his hand and jumped over the side. He took down another line from the boat to use as a search line.

Divers were lucky if the bag pile plopped down right on top of the pipeline. It was usually off a ways from the pipe. The diver would search, find the pipe and tie his guide line on it. He would inform "topside" of the direction and rough distance to the bagging spot. Then he would instruct them to tight-line the load line. He would check that it was vertical. Then he would say, "Come up easy on the load." When the bottom of the pile got about 2 or 3 feet above the sea floor, he would say, "All stop. Hold the load." He then talked with the captain and made sure they were in clear agreement on the direction and approximate distance of travel. If all was well, he would ask the captain to start "traveling". This is a very tricky and scary time for the diver. He probably thought to himself something like, "What in the hell have I gotten myself into this time."

As the bag pile moved, the diver had to shuffle-slide his feet along beside it. He had to constantly circle around it…back and forth….looking for the pipe. He always tried to keep one hand touching the bag pile as he moved around it. "Whoops, don't' go getting underneath that damn big pile of bags," might occur to the slipping diver. His free hand was out low to the side, searching. Divers have found however, that for this adventurous mission, his feet are his best pipe-finding tool. "Get those feet kick-sliding out to the side, don't let that damn pipe escape us!" or some thought like that, prodded the diver and his feet. And it does seem that many times the diver will discover the pipe by banging into it with his shins.

All pipelines first require that bags be placed under the pipe for support, before pinning-down bags are applied. Placing bags under the pipe is greatly facilitated by having an available supply of separate, individual, single bags. We had an effective technique for sending a bunch of single bags down, all grouped together in one bag pile. A big husky circular cargo net proved to be ideal. It had many strong grommets all around its perimeter. It was laid out flat on the deck and filled with a big pile of single bags. A crane hook with a large ring in it was lowered over the center of it.

The end of a long strong line was tied onto the ring. The other end was run through a grommet. It was taken back up through the ring and then down through another grommet. This was repeated until all the grommets were held by the ring. When tight-lined, the net was now a good looking sack, almost overflowing with bags. Away we go. When the diver had this creation properly positioned over an unsupported pipeline, he would make a severing cut at any safe spot on the grommet line. All the single bags would cascade down... under the pipe as well as around it. The diver still had to adjust bags under the pipe and stab in some more to make a good functional pipe underbedding. However, this operation was much sweeter for the diver than having to cut bags loose from a big all-tied-together pile, and then drag them individually over to and under the pipe.

The pipeline bagging was finally completed. Superbly so, I might add. We started bagging the legs. The project superintendent had been dismayed when we told him of the leg scours. The southwest leg had a 7 foot void under the leg bottom. The northwest leg void was over 4 feet. The east legs had about 2 or 3 foot gaps under them. This increased the menace of fast moving, corrosive, silt-laden water attacking all those pilings descending out of the bottom of the legs. There were 9 pilings evenly spaced in a circle near the outside rim of the leg bottom. Three more were in the center of the leg. It was decided we were to build a protective wall of bags on the outside of the ring of 9 pilings and to continue the wall 4 feet up the outside of the bottom of the leg.

Well, they had the bagging boys who could do it….but, at first we were not sure how. The first problem was how to get piles of bags down along the perimeters of the leg bottoms. A wide, strong walkway existed between the legs, about 15 feet below the bottom of the platform. It included walkway extensions that completely encircled each leg…and boy, did we use them. We installed two very strong, but conveniently movable air winches on the walkway directly above the area of the leg we were bagging.

For areas out of the crane's reach we often used the Shamrock. Many bag piles were placed on the boat by the crane. The Shamrock's A-frame would pick up one of the many piles on the deck and place it on the bow of the boat. The captain maneuvered the boat over against the leg, and under the tugger cable. We simply transferred the load off the boat and onto the tugger.

It was impossible to dive the low tides on the bottom. However, it was possible for the Shamrock to send bag piles down against the leg. We would put a bag pile down about 10 feet into the water, in front of the bow of the boat. We had a big strong fender secured on the bow at each side of the load-line. The bag pile was free to travel down when the Captain nosed the boat up against the leg. Later dives verified that this worked most of the time.

For this procedure, we used 1 inch diameter polypropylene line on a Shamrock winch. This allowed us to send down our homemade line cutter, which really worked well. We left the last bag pile line uncut. We transferred the boat's end of the line up to the riggers on the leg's walkway. It would eventually serve as a diver's down line.

The preferred method of diving at the platform was to tie the boat securely to the leg we were diving on. All of the bags were sent down as close to the leg as possible. A totally smooth leg, with no J-tube or valves protruding, should allow the bag pile to hit bottom down below the edge of the leg. But the terrain around the legs was rough and uneven. Bags got stuck behind a rock, others just fell back away from the leg for some unapparent reason. But, some of the bags managed to fall down almost to the outer ring of the nine platform pilings.

Bags positioned like this were the divers' helpful buddies. He would use them as, what riggers call, a "dead man" anchor. I'll call them a bag anchor. These bag anchors could help transfer the misplaced bag pile over into the needed area. A pulley was placed on the top of a usefully located anchor bag. Then a strong pull line from the surface was stabbed through that pulley and taken over to the misplaced bag pile where the end of it was secured. The diver instructed top side to tight-line the pulley line and the errant bag pile would be pulled over alongside the anchor pile to the edge of the leg.

The bag piles also had to be stabbed into the area between the two vertical diagonals where they join the leg. This proved to be a very useful place for the second tugger. The divers became quite ingenious at leading tugger wires in directions to help position the bags. Perhaps a half turn around a J-tube or pipeline would do it. A last resort was to get a choke strap and block (big pulley) to rig a fairlead around a piling.

Diving between and under Steelhead's vertical diagonal braces is probably the most dangerous diving task on the platform. If a high tide rip current suddenly attacks, the diver's hose will probably be squeezed tight against at least one brace and perhaps more. His hose can be trapped by the vertical diagonal braces, or the horizontal braces and/or worst of all, the leg. The strength of hose/brace friction is directly related to water velocity and can be so strong that even two tenders cannot pull the diver's hose. The diver himself can be pinned tightly against a brace.....trapped and almost immobile.

This happened to a diver who was working on leg A1 in the vertex area between the two vertical diagonal braces. He was checking that area to see how close it was to completion. The rest of the leg had a huge wide circle of bags extending up 4 feet above the bottom of the leg and almost completely encircling it. He descended the established down line tied-off on the pipeline J-tube. Then he trudged north along the wall of bags against the leg until he reached the north vertical diagonal brace.

So far, during the dive his hose had been well west of the platform...away from all braces. He stopped for a moment and checked what the tide was doing. Good. It was still heading north at a moderate pace. He clambered over the top of the brace and dropped down inside the gap between the two vertical diagonal braces. He dropped down further than he thought he would. It was apparent that many more bags were needed than had been realized.

He was assessing the bag situation when a strong blast of water started hitting him from the west. He knew he had felt the start of a high tide rip. The tender warned him about the rip and said it looked like it was quickly increasing velocity and to get out now! They tried to pull up his hose but it would not move....probably tight-frictioning against some brace. The diver used what free hose he had to pull himself to the top of the brace, but the blasting westerly current blew him back downwards to the bottom of the brace and still inside the vertex.

  I was the stand-by diver. Now I was the rescue diver. We got the fast cable winch ready to go. I put a big shackle into the eye at the end of it and shackled it onto my harness. I put my hand around his hose and jumped in. I began pulling myself down his hose hand over hand but the current was running so fast that I quickly wrapped both legs around his hose. This was a strong rip current. I finally got down to the lowest vertical diagonal brace and I came up against the anode that was on top of the brace. Good! It gave me a place to brace myself.

  While I took the shackle off my harness and shackled the retrieving wire around his hose, I checked his hose. It was being blasted tight against the top side of the brace I was on and also against the braces up above. I pulled it free and started messengering the retrieving shackle down to him. I kept trying to keep his hose free from the brace while I was working the shackle down. It made me remember a rescue I had witnessed….exactly like this one.

  The rescue diver tried and tried, but he simply couldn't keep the hose free enough to allow the shackle to descend it. He finally had to bring the retrieving line up and take the shackle off the hose. He had to lower the shackle wire along-side the hose, bouncing it around as best he could until it finally hit the diver. While I was thinking about that, I noticed that the current velocity was increasing. It's a struggle, but a diver can do some work in a one knot current. Two knots is a different story. The diver cannot push himself forward into it. In fact it will be trying to push him backwards. I believed the current velocity was now approaching two knots! I suddenly felt him grab the line and thankfully, too. My tender told me he was getting shackled up and to get ready.

They started winching him up. I continually felt the up/coming line and hose to make sure the lines stayed unfouled. He "wham-bammed" up alongside me! What a pleasurable whack that was! He felt my hands to make sure I had good hold of the shackle line and then up we went. The boat eased away to the west to help keep our hoses clear of braces. Numerous similar inside the vertex rescues had to be made before we completed our three year installation of the Steelhead. Some other rescues were entirely different and not quite as hazardous. Here is one that happened to me.

I had been making an inspection dive on a low horizontal when a rip current slammed into me. I tried to get back to my down line, but the opposing current wouldn't let me. Steve Stuart, my tender/diver was tending my hose on the high horizontal brace almost directly above me. He had his own down line. When the tender told him my dilemma, he went right into action. He had my hose in his hand and told us all what he wanted to do. We did it. The tender on deck tightlined my hose. Steve unshackled his down line from the sacrificial anode next to him and shackled it to his harness. Down my tight hose he came. He shackled his down line to the anode next to us and up that line we went. When we got out I thanked him for his good, quick-action rescue. "You'd have done the same for me," he said and of course he was right. We were all true, proven comrades of the Inlet.

Steve and I performed an identical Steelhead inspection during a time when pile driving was being done on deck. This terrible sound is bad enough when on the deck, but in water it is magnified many times more powerfully. We arranged to tell the pile driver men when we were going to dive and they agreed not drive pile at dive time. They forgot! Steve was tending my hose from the upper brace. I was inspecting the lower brace almost directly below him. Suddenly, the chaotic, bedlam noise of pile driving attacked us. The terrible roaring noise created an overwhelming wild feeling of instant crazy insanity! I couldn't even think straight. I yelled for Steve to pull me up and away I went. Steve had stayed right there for me. When I got to him, we both shot to the surface. Serious, emphatic discussions were held. They never forgot to make sure we weren't in the water again.

On Nov. 3, 1987, the last dive of the year was made. The ice drove us out. We had accomplished a lot but there was still more to do. All the pipelines had been bag/stabilized and most of the braces had been inspected. Three of the four legs had been fully bagged…underneath and up the sides of the legs.

After we divers left, drilling began on leg B-1, the northwest leg. The driller watching the mud pit suddenly saw a huge amount of gas bubbles boiling up out of the mud pit, a scary indicator of an imminent explosion! He sounded the alarm. There was superfast life boat launching action and barely in time. There was a tremendous, catastrophic explosion, but fortunately, no one was seriously injured.

The Grayling platform was two/thirds of a mile away to the northwest and received a Danger Alert call from the Steelhead. Some of the crew rushed out to a good viewing spot on the platform. Leg B-1 was directly in front of them and they all watched it intently. Suddenly they saw a huge fire ball shooting upward and they were staggered by the tremendous roar and ferocity of the accompanying explosion.

Not long after this happened, a Steelhead platform executive asked me to come out to the Steelhead for a meeting. A group of us were taken out to the platform in a helicopter. The northwest leg looked like some WWII bomb blasts. I got out of the chopper and walked carefully through all the debris over to the leg. What destruction! Bent and twisted hardware everywhere. Things were just blown apart. One big H-beam especially impressed me. In the process of being totally blown away from what it supported, it had been sort of mutilated. The ragged severed end had been bent way over at an angle and had also been crunched...sort of flattened out looking. There was debris everywhere, but the northwest leg had obviously borne the brunt of it.

The conference was mainly concerned with describing all the damages that had been done, and potential repairs. An inventory of the platform deck revealed that a lot of equipment was missing.

Was it simply blown to pieces or was it blown over the side? I was asked about the Shamrock's ability to retrieve heavy, bulky objects. I explained that the Shamrock's A-frame could lift heavy things off bottom. However, getting them out of the water would be difficult. It would be better to keep the object on our winch line at the water's surface. Then we could travel over under a crane and transfer the load without having to lift it out of the water. If an object was on top of a pipeline, we could simply use the boat's winch to pick it off the pipe. Then we would move the boat well off to the side before lowering it down and cutting the object loose.

They were pleased that the Shamrock could do all this because they were concerned about having to get a small derrick barge. This brought us around to our foreseeable diving missions. Of course they would want full platform and pipeline inspections. Some blown up things were bound to have landed on braces and pipelines. Most of the drilling derrick on the platform must have been blown over the side. The four lattice work sides of the derrick were light metal, not heavy H-beams and hopefully the Shamrock could pick them up.

An impressive array of diver challenges were starting to be revealed. There was also concern about the condition of leg B1's twelve supporting piling. A drill ship would be anchored alongside the platform in July to drill a relief well. It was assumed that we would do the required diving, however we would not start diving until late August.

Bill Morterud and I were the divers on the drill ship. It was the usual stuff: setting the base plate and stabbing the drill pipe into the hole. The drill ship was anchored up in 205 feet of water, 5 feet deeper than Steelhead, but neither of us wanted to consider whether the nitrogen narcosis was a little worse than at Steelhead. We discovered that it was.

This diving job did reveal a wonderful invention to us, though. The ship had a sonar depth gauge which was coupled to a current velocity meter. Just dial in the depth of interest, and the meter would tell you the water currents, direction and velocity at that depth. Our diving company got one for us immediately. What a stupendous gift for us Inlet divers.

The first Steelhead inspection diving of 1988 was done on the bottom of leg B1. The divers began a thorough blind man's inspection. Large pieces of blown apart equipment, H-beams, pipes of all sizes, big hunks of grating were scattered around on the bottom like a dumped out bag of children's toys. The blasted out hole under the leg was about 20 feet deep. When we were down in the hole we were diving in 220 feet of water. The nitrogen narcosis was very noticeably stronger and oppressive. We had to work harder to maintain our concentration levels....in fact, all thought processes.

The twelve pilings felt like they had been shot by slugs from many 10 gauge shotguns, but it must have been the flying gravel. The indentations were about a ½ inch diameter and penetrated approximately ½ inch into the metal. When the engineers heard this news they immediately ordered a supply of cylindrical piling that were a proper diameter to be driven down inside the existing ones. The engineers wanted super reinforcement. The original pilings were driven 135 feet into the sea floor. The inner pilings were driven much deeper-many hundreds of feet deeper.

After we finished checking the pilings, we began roaming around leg B1. Debris was plentiful. As we explored the debris field, we realized it was not simply confined to leg B1. It extended to leg A1 and even further south and west. The debris field on the A1 pipeline began about 50 feet out from the leg and extended at least 150 feet down the pipe. The A2 pipeline was parallel to the A1 and only about 10 or 15 feet south of it. Sure enough, it had debris for about the same length of span as A1 did, at least 150 feet and exactly opposite to it. There was all kinds of hardware alongside and on top of the pipelines. Much of it was big. The debris consisted of fairly long 6 or 8 inch diameter pipes. They were heavy and we assumed they were drill pipes. Also there were long lengths of tubing. Some impressive size H-beams were laying alongside the pipe and on top of it. Some had hit the pipeline with a force that tore off long lengths of the pipe's layer of protective insulation, leaving only the bare pipe. A drill pipe was found alongside a pipeline that had 7 feet of similar damage.

Wow! This was becoming a tour of a valuable, torn-up million dollar junk yard!

The divers began the task of lifting up and removing every possible invader from atop the pipelines. We coiled up and removed hundreds of feet of 1 inch cable laying all over the pipelines. It was probably the derrick's block and tackle rigging cable. Some things, especially H-beams, were just too heavy even for us strong-arm divers. We picked these off with the crane line.

We discovered a lot of new scouring underneath the pipelines. One was 60 feet long. Another was 70 feet long. The 20 foot hole under leg B1 illustrated the powerful upheaval force the blast exerted against the sea floor. A lot of the scouring was 3 feet deep. We began an ambitious bagging program. We were sure grateful that the platform crane could reach out to all the bagging locations. .

We also had another mission injected into our schedule. From Sept 23 until Oct. 15, our high tide diving chores also included baby- sitting the tow boats bringing huge barge loads of gravel to dump in the hole under leg B1. The Shamrock crew watched the tide action for them. We also helped to maneuver the dump barge into position at the optimum time. We all did a good job. In 3 weeks the dump barges completely filled that wide 20 foot deep hole with 60,000 tons of gravel. (The tonnage information was provided by the Cook Inlet Regional Citizens Advisory Council.) While the pipeline bagging was going on, we inspected the west side of the platform. Surprisingly the west side braces appeared undamaged. Flooded member readings were taken on west braces and they were all dry. A few small dents were found on the west low horizontal, but the brace had not been punctured.

On Oct. 15, the last gravel dump was made and our diving repairs mission was pretty well completed. But there were still newly scoured out areas we could work on. However, the platform needed a lot of replacement equipment and repair work. Supply boats would be journeying back and forth to the platform for quite a while. They didn't need our dive boat getting in their way and using the crane time. So on October 18th, the Shamrock and her divers departed until next years' dive season began.

The winter of 1988-1989 had been especially cold. When we arrived on Steelhead in spring '89, we learned that the platform had been severely battered, probably by a colliding ice berg. I immediately remembered when the whole south horizontal brace on Shell A had been torn away by an ice berg in 1971. We began our inspection of Steelhead with trepidation.

I began the inspection of Steelhead by looking at the north upper horizontal brace. Amazingly, half a dozen sacrificial anodes had been completely torn away! They had been replaced by numerous big dents-about two foot long by 5 inches deep. Other anodes and braces had also been damaged, but all the braces were intact and dry---no flooding. We completed all of the required Inspections and sand bag missions including the complete bagging of leg A2.

Steelhead's halting installation had finally been completed! Thank you for your interest in our truly monumental project...and all the other diving projects I've enjoyed describing to you, the reader.

Outstanding Cook Inlet Divers and Crew who have worked on many platforms over the years.

From left to right: Gene Cleary, Jiggs Jackson, Monty McPherson, Steve Stuart, Gary Kalpakoff, myself, and John Daly. Eddie Mata, top row.

ABOUT THE AUTHOR

I had a free, unleashed childhood.... My father was a lawyer, my mother stayed home...and, fortunately, they weren't the hovering type, so I had an adventurous, roaming, Tom Sawyer boyhood... for which I am deeply grateful as confidence in my own abilities developed. The family expectation was college, becoming a doctor was encouraged. But after three years of college the lure of that diver, ready to jump overboard, called to me.

I left home and hitchhiked to Oregon to work as a choker setter in the woods, planning to use the money to go to diving school. This was work which taught me many skills, such as wire splicing and rigging....skills which turned out to be relevant later to diving. After 3 months in the woods, I went to California to look into a commercial dive school, which, to my disappointment had misrepresented itself.

However, shifting my gears for the time being, an ad in the paper caught my eye which promised that a course in celestial navigation could lead to a career as a navigator on a tuna clipper. I signed up and learned to use a sextant to locate a ship's position the way navigators had done for centuries by using the sun, planets and the stars. My instructor made a personal rocommendation attesting to my navigational abilities to the owner of the tuna clipper, the Irene S and to its skipper, Captain Magellan. I spent almost three months navigating the Irene S in the Pacific Ocean off the coast of Mexico and Central America.   This has remained one of the highlights of my life.

During the early fifties, I married, had a child, settling down in Hermosa Beach, California. I met Mel Fisher at his dive shop in Redondo Beach and worked weekends for him as a certified diving instructor, taking the fledging divers to Catalina Island and other off shore islands. I supported my family by technical writing for Douglas aircraft, but the goal of going to commercial dive school was never far from my mind and in 1960, I got my chance.

A well-known and highly respected commercial diver, Art Broman, had opened a commercial dive school. Due to a terrible accident, he was no longer able to dive. He had been working on a big, long diving job, laying a pipeline out into deep water. He was taking a lengthy decompression in a chamber on the deck of the barge. The crane swung a heavy load around and accidentally crashed it into Art's chamber, breaking it open. The sudden complete decompression caused an immediate and tremendous case of the bends.

Art eventually recovered enough, while waiting for his settlement money, to open a commercial diving school. I was fortunate to be one of his first students. It could not have been greater for me. He excelled at teaching diving. One of his specialties was using the underwater cutting torch. He could cut big thick metal plates in half....blindfolded and in total darkness! Best of all, he taught his students this skill. This gave me a taste of what I was in for diving in the Cook Inlet. I have always been grateful to my friend and teacher, Art Broman.

I joined the local Piledrivers and Divers Union and began going out on jobs as a rigger, tender and then working into more and more diving, mostly in the local South Bay area. Over those 5 years, I met some outstanding men. Gene Cleary and Jiggs Jackson became both friends and partners, relationships which lasted through their lifetimes. When the first platforms were towed to the Cook Inlet, it was a natural progression for many of us to follow the work to Alaska. I packed up my family, which by now included three more children, and followed Gene to Alaska and began my 40 years as an Alaskan diver.

I am proud of my log books. They are clear and concise. All the pertinent information is there. Maybe not meticulous, but the essential details are there. When unusual things happened, though, I wrote more expansively…especially when the events I call "The Hazardous Adventures" occurred. In forty years of diving the Inlet, I still have 95% of all the log books I ever wrote. When I read them now, I'm surprised at the interesting events I'd forgotten.

In 1965, Gene, Jiggs and I worked for Associated Divers of Alaska. We worked furiously for 5 years, through the summer of 1970 installing numerous platforms and their associated pipelines. Then, suddenly, we realized that the diving work was completed and all the platforms were in and nothing else was on the horizon. Diving jobs had disappeared in the Inlet.

Dick Evans Divers, a diving company from Louisiana which had worked also in the Inlet during these years, offered me a job coming up in the Bay of Fundy, St. John, Canada. I was hired as lead diver for this job. The tidal action is almost identical to the Cook Inlet with one interesting difference. The high tides are even more extreme than the Inlet tides. A high tide can be 50 feet compared to the lowly 36 feet in the Cook Inlet! Intrigued by this and needing to work, my wife and I packed up the four kids and the dog in our red, 69 VW bus with our canoe on top and drove to New Orleans. I dived out in the Gulf of Mexico until the job in the Bay of Fundy started. I worked five months in the Bay of Fundy showing the New Orleans divers all I had learned about treacherous tidal water diving. The company really appreciated my expertise, which made me feel proud!

In 1971, Gene Cleary called me back to Alaska.....work was picking up in the Inlet. He had started his own dive company, Cleary Diving, and wanted me to come home and work for him. New platforms were being installed, repairs needed to the existing ones and new work needed on all of them. Sea water electrolysis was attacking all the metal in the Inlet. As a result, we installed big protective anode sleds around all the platforms. We also assisted oil exploration operations in the Beaufort Sea, Alaska's most northern water. These were busy years for me.

Gene sold his company in 1978 to Martech Alaska, and I worked for them as lead diver and boy, did we go to work. Martech put in bids all over the state, winning jobs that took me from working in the Inlet providing oil drilling support, to diving on jack-up rigs in the Bering Sea and the Gulf of Alaska. I also went to work for Martech in Seattle, diving in Seattle Harbor installing a big out-fall line. Best of all, for a cold Alaskan diver, I was sent to Honolulu to repair a pipeline. I worked there with a great local diver, Marc Stearns. In 1986, Martech was awarded the diving on the new Steelhead platform which was going to stand in 200 feet of water and began drilling in 1987.

In 1992, my old friend, Jiggs Jackson was hired as diving supervisor on the 3rd Harbor Tunnel in Boston. He asked me to join him and I gladly hired on. Our children were grown, in college, or working, so once again, my wife and I picked up stakes and just the two of us moved to Boston. The diving on the tunnel was finished in 1994 and we returned home to Alaska.

By this time, American Marine had bought Martech Alaska. I worked for American Marine from 1995 to 2007 when I retired at 75. These were some of the most productive and satisfying years of my diving career. American Marine has always hired really top, professional people who always backed their men 100%, making sure we had the equipment or support we needed. Scott Vuillemot, the owner and Tom Ulrich the Alaska supervisor, are outstanding people to work for. We always try to go to American Marine's Christmas parties. It's wonderful to fraternize with old comrades.